Miles Lassiter

(circa 1777-1850)
An Early African-American Quaker from
Lassiter Mill, Randolph County, North
Carolina: My Research Journey to Home

Margo Lee Williams

Backintyme
Palm Coast, Florida U.S.A.

© 2011 Margo Lee Williams
ALL RIGHTS RESERVED

Published by Backintyme,
A subsidiary of Boxes and Arrows, Inc.

Backintyme Publishing
30 Medford Drive
Palm Coast FL 32137-2504

phone: 860-468-9631
email: sales@backintyme.com
website: http://backintyme.com/publishing.php

ISBN: 978-0939479-382
Printed in the United States of America
Library of Congress Control Number: 2011941307

To my mother, Margaret Lee Williams,
who gave me the past,
and to my daughter, Turquoise Lee Williams,
who promises the future.

Contents

Acknowledgments	ix
Preface	xi
Introduction	xiii

I	**My Search for My Family**	**1**
1	**Grandma Ellen**	**3**
	Memories	4
	Starting the Research	7
	Division of Lands of Miles Lassiter	11
	Randolph County Historical Society	14
2	**On the Road to Randolph County**	**17**
	Randolph County Roots	18
	The Drive South	20
	Kate and the Family	20
	The Lassiter Mill Community	23
	The White Lassiters	24
	Church and Family	27
3	**Tracing the Land**	**33**
	Hildy	33
	Estate of Healy Phillips or Lassiter	34

	Other Records	37
	Miles and Healy, Husband and Wife	38
4	**Life in Pre-Civil War Randolph County**	**41**
	Slave or Free	42
	The Lassiter Slaves	42
	Black Codes and Randolph County	43
	Education and Religion	46
	Quakers and Back Creek Friends	48
	Property	49
	Marriage between slaves and free people	51
	Restrictions	52
5	**The People on the Land**	**55**
	The Heirs of Healy Phillips	55
	The Genealogical Journal	57
	The County Library	58
	The Final Decree	59
6	**Family Reunions and Private Papers**	**63**
	The First Reunion	63
	Letters and Deeds	65
	The Second Reunion	70
7	**Still Looking**	**71**
	Emsley Lassiter	72
	The Other Children	73
8	**Back to the Land**	**75**
	Due to Bonds	75
	Land Values and Money	77
	Putting It Together	78
9	**You Never Know**	**81**
	An Obituary	82
	Sarah Lassiter's Family Revisited	83
	Miles as Slave Revisited	86

CONTENTS

Blood Relations	87
Sold Into Freedom	90
The Land Revisited	91
Miles' final years as a Quaker	92

10 It's Never Finished   **97**

II   A Genealogical Record   **101**

11 Some Descendants of Miles Lassiter   **103**
    The First Generation   105
    The Second Generation   120

List of Figures

1.1 Margaret Lee Williams 3
1.2 Louise Phillips and Elinora Lee 5
1.3 Margaret and Verna Lee 6
1.4 Nancy Dunson 1860 census 9
1.5 Ellen Mayo Deed to Will Lassiter 12
1.6 Miles' 1815 Deed 13
1.7 Lassiter Family 1900 15

2.1 Randolph County NC Map 17
2.2 Uwharrie River behind Lassiter's Mill 19
2.3 Lassiter Family home 21
2.4 Margaret Lee Williams and Kate Lassiter Jones 22
2.5 Margaret Williams at A & T University 23
2.6 Lassiter's Mill, 1982 25
2.7 Strieby Congregational UCC Church, 1982 . . 27
2.8 Strieby Church Cemetery, 1982 28
2.9 Home of Arthur Hill, Strieby, NC, 1982 29
2.10 Margaret Williams on Old Salisbury St., 1982 . 30
2.11 St. Sardis 31
2.12 First Congregational Church, 1982 31

3.1 Ellen Dunson Smitherman Mayo land 33
3.2 Heley Phillips 1840 census 36
3.3 Ezekiel Lassiter Letters of Administration . . . 37

4.1 North Carolina Manumission Society Flyer . . 41

5.1	Descendants of Miles and Healy Lassiter	55
5.2	Nancy Dunson grave marker	59
5.3	Division of Lands of Miles Lassiter	61
6.1	Lassiter Family Reunion, 1987	63
6.2	Harold Lassiter	66
6.3	Lassiter Family Reunion, 1996	70
7.1	Emsley Lassiter 1880 census Indiana	71
8.1	The old barn, Lassiter family farm	75
9.1	Miles' obituary	81
10.1	Vella Lassiter, Margaret Williams, Will Lassiter	97
10.2	Margo and Turquoise Williams	99
11.1	Abigail Phillips Lassiter ceramic pot	106
11.2	Granny Kate Polk Lassiter	110
11.3	Descendants of Colier Lassiter, 1982	121
11.4	Alice Lassiter Speed and Margaret L. Williams	122
11.5	Ulysses Winston Lassiter	123
11.6	Julia Ann Lassiter Sanders and daughter	125
11.7	Julia Ann and Thomas E. Lassiter	127
11.8	Roxanne Smitherman Waddell Wilburn	128
11.9	Oddfellows Cemetery, Asheboro NC, 1982	129

Acknowledgments

There are many people to acknowledge for their assistance in developing this account of the Lassiter family tradition. First, I must thank my mother, Margaret Lee Williams, whose memories of her maternal ancestors, especially those of her great grandmother, Ellen Dunson Smitherman Mayo (Grandma Ellen), inspired my search.

Second, I must acknowledge the late Kate Lassiter Jones, the late Harold Lassiter and Aveus (Ave) Lassiter Edmundson for their help, their incredible knowledge not only of the family history, but also of the county history, and for their unconditional acceptance of their previously unknown cousin. In addition, I am so very appreciative of Harold's willingness to share the precious family papers and pictures for which he has so faithfully cared. Then there are all the other cousins who have allowed me to question them about their lives and their families, and who provided pictures, names of descendants and addresses.

I am especially grateful to the late Carolyn Neely Hager, the wonderful county librarian who was my first real contact with Randolph County. Her interest and enthusiasm for my search, her knowledge of the county (its history and residents), and her friendship, continually encouraged me.

I would be remiss if I did not also thank the many people who helped me learn the field of genealogy, especially Donald Barnes, the late Jimmy Walker, and Joyce Candland. Each introduced me to three important organizations: the Genealogy Club of the Montgomery County (Maryland) Historical Society; the Afro-American Historical and Genealogical Society; and the local Family History Centers of the Family History Library in Salt Lake City, Utah, respectively.

I am deeply indebted to the late Shirley King, Victoria Price, Theresa Rector, Janis Steenberg, Luis Zapata and Vernon Skinner for their editorial assistance. Their comments, observations, and suggestions were enormously helpful.

Preface

When I began this research, I did not know that Miles Lassiter was an early African-American Quaker in the state of North Carolina. In fact, I did not know he was my ancestor, nor even that I had any Lassiter ancestors. I was trying to learn more about my mother's family—especially her great grandmother.

That quest has given me more than history. In many ways it gave me the extended family I did not have while growing up, as well as a legacy to pass on to my child. As often happens over time, especially as families move about, my immediate family was no longer in touch with other branches of the extended family in North Carolina, so I had not known the Lassiter family until I began my research. On the other hand, many of the family members who continued to be in touch with each other only knew that they were related, but were no longer sure how the various branches of the family fit together. Thus, this research journey has given each of us something precious.

With regard to Miles and his place in both Quaker and North Carolina history, he too has been somewhat lost to both. I hope that this book can make a contribution not only to genealogy, but also serve to remind all of us that while traditional history texts recount the grand events and talk about the big personalities, true history is made up of everyday people who do extraordinary things quietly, not even realizing that they have made a mark on history.

As it turns out, this family's members have gone on to do many extraordinary things, some of which I have been able to

relate herein, and others which are still waiting to be discovered.
— Margo Lee Williams

Introduction

Like many family histories, this family history, my history, begins with an oral accounting handed down by my mother. My mother had heard various stories during her growing up years, and remembered some of them, and then during my childhood she told them to me. However, generally, when probing for more information, she would say that she didn't really know anything. She wasn't aware of any family left in North Carolina, and the few cousins she knew who lived in Baltimore, were no longer in touch. Although she did have one cousin, living not too far from us, who was married, but had no children, we had little contact with her during my childhood. My mother considered herself to be a person with no family other than her sister, her husband (my father), and me. Her stories peaked my interest, however—stories about her grandmother, her grandmother's sisters, their families, and her great grandmother, Ellen, who lived "up the Plank Road," in Asheboro (Randolph County), North Carolina. I was curious about them. I wondered what had become of them. Surely there must be someone...

By the mid 1970s, I had learned about Alex Haley's pursuit of his ancestors, and subsequent publication of his book, *Roots*. What I learned from reading about his research, and hearing him explain about it on the Tonight Show with Johnny Carson, was that I, too, could do this kind of research on my family. It was during that appearance that I first learned about the Family History Library in Salt Lake City, Utah, and its local genealogy libraries (now called Family History Centers), which were open to the public.

The realization that I could, in fact, research my family's history myself became even stronger when I moved to Washington, D.C., and discovered that some of the most important research facilities for doing genealogy were located here, especially the National Archives and the Library of Congress. However, it was the purchase of my first how-to book that actually helped me get started with serious genealogical research in an effort to corroborate and expand on the stories my mother had told me. Armed with, and guided by that book, I set out to learn more about the family of which my mother knew relatively little.

While the book was helpful, I knew I needed more guidance. There came a great opportunity when a parishioner in my congregation (Donald Barnes, C.G.) arranged to teach a beginning genealogy class at our church. That inspired me to take other courses offered by my local county genealogical society, the Genealogy Club of the Montgomery County Historical Society (Rockville, Maryland). Soon, I was attending other workshops and subscribing to journals. I learned many important lessons and keys to doing genealogical research. One important lesson was not to jump to conclusions based on one or only a few documents. They can be the basis of a working hypothesis, but one has to keep looking for documents to support it, and be aware of, and consider carefully all possible scenarios. What may seem to be the story at a given time may change dramatically as new information comes to light. In addition, a family's story may never be completely uncovered because of missing records: records lost; records burned or otherwise destroyed; records misplaced or misfiled; and records never formally filed. Then there are the family secrets, or cover stories, which may have misrepresented the facts, and over time distorted the family history.

I had a reasonable amount of success early on with my research, and was quickly able to extend my mother's family tree back two more generations beyond Grandma Ellen, to her grandfather, Miles Lassiter. In that process I learned about property Grandma Ellen owned. This was not the property on the Plank Road. That property, I discovered, actually belonged to her second husband, Charles Mayo. Her property seemed to be in the country, along the Uwharrie River. It was a piece of land referred to as part of the "Division of Lands of Miles Lassiter." It became the principal source of and key to my family's genealogy and its history—a history that stretched back to colonial days, and the time of the War of Independence. That property led me to heretofore unknown cousins who would provide me with many pieces of information about family members, such as the habit of switching first for middle names, and then sometimes back again, or the use of nicknames. More importantly, it led me to the community in which Miles and his descendants lived, a community in which I have my roots, Lassiter Mill, (New Hope Township) Randolph County, North Carolina.

This book tells this story in two parts. The first part will tell the story of my research journey. Included in this part will be a brief history and discussion of the socio-economic-political background of Randolph County during Miles' lifetime. Because this is intended to be only a brief sketch and backdrop for subsequent research discussions, it relies heavily on the work of John Hope Franklin's book *The Free Negro in North Carolina, 1790-1860*. Out of this research has emerged a biography of what is known about Miles Lassiter's life, a story that could readily provide the backdrop for an historical novel. Such research journeys and the stories they tell are vital to the effort to lift up, celebrate, and give honor to those lives that have been ignored, and thereby marginalized, by so-called mainstream historians—the individual people of color, euphemistically referred to as minorities. The second part will provide a genealogical report of Miles' descendants, and includes brief biographical sketches of his children.

Part I

My Search for My Family

Chapter 1

Grandma Ellen

Figure 1.1: Margaret Lee Williams, my mother

Memories

My research on my family actually began with a search for information on the ancestry of my mother's great grandmother, Ellen Mayo. My mother, Margaret, told me about her many memories of her Grandma Ellen, and the visits she made to her house and large farm "up the old Plank Road," which was then outside the town of Asheboro, Randolph County, North Carolina.

It was a large, one-story house. According to my mother, there was a big living room, big dining room, big kitchen, big fireplace. Everything was big. The house had three bedrooms, and a bathroom. Not a bathroom like ours today, but a room where one would take a bath, with a large tin tub that had to be taken out back in order to be emptied. There was a front porch, and a smaller back porch. There was a smokehouse, a large tub out back in which clothes and sheets were boiled on washday, and a two-seater outhouse. There was a private company whose job it was to empty and clean out the outhouse, making sure it had clean water in it.

My mother said that Grandma Ellen and her husband, Grandpa Charles Mayo (not my mother's biological great grandfather), grew corn, wheat, potatoes. and peanuts, which Grandpa Charles loved. They also had pigs and many chickens. My mother remembered that when she visited Grandma Ellen, she kept a large bowl on the table filled high with eggs. People without chickens, both Whites and non-Whites, would come to buy eggs from Grandma Ellen. My mother also remembered that Grandma Ellen had a beautiful horse-drawn buggy with fringe—the proverbial surrey with the fringe on top that I sang about in music class at school when growing up. They had a horse used only on Sundays to pull the surrey to church or visiting. My mother noted that motor vehicles were becoming popular at the time. Grandma Ellen would watch these vehicles passing by, and marvel at them. They were one of the many things heralding a new generation. However, she did not

Figure 1.2: Louise Smitherman Phillips and Elinora Phillips Lee circa 1915

understand the pronunciation of the term being used for them, *mobiles*, so she would say to her daugher, "Louise, look at the mobees! Look at all the mobees!"

In 1920, Grandma Ellen suffered a stroke. My mother told me that she, her sister Vern, and her grandmother (Ellen's daughter Mary Louise, called *Louise*, but whom they called *Mama*) went to Asheboro to help care for her. My mother and her sister were living with their grandmother Mama Louise at the time because Elinora, their mother and Louise's daughter, had died on Armistice Day, 1918, in the great Swine

Flu epidemic. Grandma Ellen died within two weeks of their arrival. At first Louise, my mother and Vern stayed on with Charlie Mayo, but he and Louise did not get along well. "He was stingy," according to my mother, so Louise, my mother, and Vern moved to the house that Louise owned on Salisbury Street.

Figure 1.3: Margaret and Verna Lee, circa 1920

Salisbury Street was inside the town limits of Asheboro, and was paved with gravel and cobblestone. Louise grew corn and wheat on the land behind her house. She hired the husband of her niece, Eliza Phillips Walker, to plant, care for, and harvest the corn and wheat. Louise proceeded to renovate the house, which had been rented out for a few years. About two years later however, Louise's children, who lived in New York and New Jersey, begged her to move back north. She did so around 1923, after marrying John Ingram, her third husband. She took my mother and Vern with her, since she was their guardian.

Starting the Research

My mother remembered all of these things about Grandma Ellen and her farm. She also recalled that Charlie Mayo was Grandma Ellen's second husband, and that Smitherman was the surname of her first husband, but she did not know Ellen's maiden name, nor the names of her parents. Therefore, in one of my first efforts to find out more about her family, I requested a copy of Grandma Ellen's death certificate from the state of North Carolina. It showed that her parents' names were Calvin Dunston and Nancy Lassiter.[1] I had never heard either name before, and when I questioned my mother, she hadn't either. A search of census records for Randolph County, North Carolina, at the National Archives revealed the following:

- In 1880, a Nancy Dunson was listed as head of household with some of her children and grandchildren, but Ellen was not among them;[2]

- In 1870, Calvin and Nancy Dunson were listed with children, but no Ellen;[3]

---

[1] North Carolina Death Certificate #16225-404, Ellen Dunson, Certificate in possession of the author. See also Randolph County Death Record Book 7:6, F(amily) H(istory) L(ibrary) M(icrofilm) #0475244.

[2] 1880 US Census, population schedule, Randolph County, North Carolina, Nancy Dunson, New Hope Township, S.D. 2, E.D. 223, p. 1, dwelling 2, family 3. NAM #T9-978.

[3] 1870 US Census, population schedule, Randolph County, North Carolina, Calvin Dunson, New Hope Township, P.O. Lassiter's Mill, p. 10, line 9, dwelling 80, family 83. NAM #M593-1156.

- In 1860, there was a Calvin Dunson and Nancy with children, including an Ellen;[4] and

- In 1850, a Miles Lassiter was head of household, with Samuel, Parthana, Colier, Abigail, Nancy and Jane Lassiter, and a John Phillips included therein.[5]

I learned three things from this census search: first, there were at least two spellings for the last name, Dunson and Dunston; second, it appeared that it was probably Grandma Ellen who was recorded living with her parents in 1860, and third, it was probably Grandma Ellen's mother, Nancy, who was recorded in the 1850 census living in the household of her father with at least some of her siblings.

This was the first time I had come across the name *Miles Lassiter*.' Although there was another household of free Lassiters of color listed in the 1850 census, Miles' household was the only one with a Nancy. The other would turn out to be that of Miles' son, Wiley. This was an exciting find! Grandma Ellen's family was a free family of color, dating back at least to the 1850s. I reported this information to my mother. She remembered that her grandmother, Louise, had told her that their family had been free, not slaves, but my mother thought she didn't know what she was talking about. After all, everyone knew slavery didn't end until the Civil War was over, so how could they be free? Well, she mused, her grandmother wasn't so crazy after all.

Efforts to locate a marriage record for Nancy Lassiter and Calvin Dunston proved fruitless, possibly because they had a

---

[4] 1860 US Census, free schedule, Randolph County, North Carolina, Calvin Dunson, West Division, P.O. Asheboro, p. 148, line 17, dwelling 1098, family 1083. NAM #M653-910.

[5] 1850 US Census, free schedule, Randolph County, North Carolina, Miles Lassiter, Ashborough Township, Southern Division, p. 136, dwelling 808 (803), family 817 (811). It says that Miles, Samuel and Jane can read and write. N(ational) A(rchives) M(icrofilm) #M432-641, and FHLM #444654, item 2.

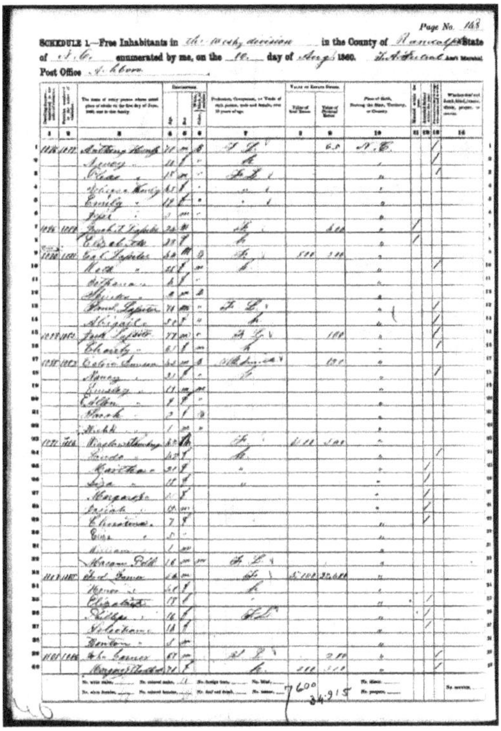
Page No. 168

SCHEDULE 1.—Free Inhabitants in ... in the County of ... State of ... enumerated by me, on the ... day of ... 1860. ... Ass't Marshal.

Post Office ...

Figure 1.4: Nancy Dunson 1860 census

common law marriage. However, this did not seem likely, since Nancy's older brother, Colier had legally married, and her husband, Calvin, had married his first wife legally in Wake County before coming to Randolph County. Later, I learned that during this time one could marry by publishing banns, that is, by announcing in a church service (I wonder what church?) that a particular couple planned to wed, and asking if there were any people who had objections. This was usually done three weeks in a row, and if no one objected, the couple could marry. These banns were not registered with the county officials the way the later marriage bonds and licenses were. On the other hand, it was also true that not all records from the time period had survived.

I learned from correspondence with the Randolph County Courthouse that Ellen Dunson married Anderson Smitherman in 1865 in Randolph County.[6] I went back to the National Archives to look at the census records. They showed that:

- Ellen, her husband, Anderson Smitherman, and children (including Louise) were living in Randolph County in 1870[7] and 1880[8];

- In 1900, Anderson Smitherman continued to live in Randolph County,[9] but Ellen was not with him;

- While a search of Randolph County for Ellen with her second husband, Charles Mayo, found nothing, a search of neighboring Guilford County showed that Ellen (Hellen) and Charles Mayo were living there[10]; and finally,

- By the 1910 census, Ellen and Charles Mayo were again living in Randolph County.[11]

---

[6] Anderson Smitherman and Ellen Dunson, Marriage Book 2:71. Certified copy. See also Randolph County Marriage Registers, 1851-1901, FHLM #0475239; Index to Marriages—Men, FHLM #0475241; or Index to Marriages—Women FHLM #0475240. In addition, all of the marriages for this time period have been published by *The Genealogical Journal* by the Randolph County Genealogical Society.

[7] 1870 US Census, population schedule, Randolph County, North Carolina, Anderson Smitherman, Union Township, P.O. Asheboro, p. 9, line 1, dwelling and family 63. NAM #M593-1156.

[8] 1880 US Census, population schedule, Randolph County, North Carolina, Anderson Smitherman, New Hope Township, S.D. 2, E.D. 223, p. 3 [stamped p. 185], dwelling 18, family 20. NAM #T9-978.

[9] 1900 US Census, population schedule, Randolph County, North Carolina, Anderson Smitherman, Asheboro Township, volume 54, E.D. 79, Sheet 3, line 60, "servant", enumerated with John M. Clark. NAM #T623-1212.

[10] 1900 US Census, population schedule, Guilford County, North Carolina, Charles Mayo, Moorehead Township, (vol 31), sheet 4, E.D. 65, line 92. NAM #T623-1128. Unfortunately no marriage record for this marriage has been located, the Guilford County marriage records for this time period are incomplete with many missing entries.

[11] 1910 US Census, population schedule, Randolph County, North Car-

Grandma Ellen 11

I was delighted. I had found Grandma Ellen, her husband, Anderson Smitherman (my great- great grandfather), and my great grandmother, Louise, in the census, as well as Grandma Ellen with her second husband, Charles Mayo, the man my mother knew as a child. My mother never met Anderson Smitherman because he died before she was born.

Division of Lands of Miles Lassiter

I wanted to find out more about Ellen's house on the Plank Road. I wondered if the deed would reveal any additional information about her ancestry. Perhaps the property originated with her family. I made a request to the Register of Deeds for Randolph County, for deeds registered to Ellen Mayo. The Register returned two deeds. Descriptions of the land also included information that Ellen's ownership of the land originated in the *Division of Lands of Miles Lassiter, Superior Court File #7385.*[12]

These two deeds showed that Ellen sold this inherited land to Will and Colon Lassiter. I had seen the name of Will Lassiter, the young son of Winston and Ora (Kearns) Lassiter. on the 1900 census. Winston was the youngest son of Colier and Katie Lassiter, and Colier was enumerated in Miles' household in 1850, along with Nancy. It was looking like Nancy and Colier were brother and sister, making Ellen, Will and Colon most likely cousins. In any event, neither of these deeds was for property on the Plank Road. I learned later that the property belonged to Charlie Mayo. These deeds seemed to refer to land elsewhere in the county.

My requests to both the Randolph County Courthouse and

---

olina, Charles Mayho, Asheboro Township, S.D. 7, E.D.76, Sheet 22B. NAM #624-1128.

[12] Estate of Miles Lassiter/Charles and Ellen Mayo to Will Lassiter and Colon Lassiter, Deed Book 166:91, FHLM #0470286; and Colon C. Lassiter to Ellen Mayo, Deed Book 163:264, FHLM #0470285.

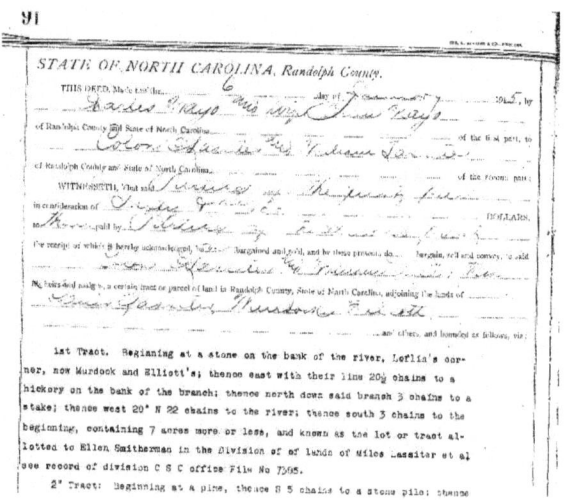

Figure 1.5: Ellen Mayo Deed to Will Lassiter

the North Carolina State Archives for any record of such a division of lands were not productive because no file or file number could be located under the name of Miles Lassiter. By this time I had become familiar with the use of the microfilmed resources of the Family History Centers (locally based libraries where one can borrow microfilmed and microfiched records from the Family History Library in Salt Lake City, Utah). At my local Family History Center, I searched microfilmed records of Equity records and the probate index, but these yielded no information about inherited property belonging to Miles Lassiter.

My continued efforts to identify property in Miles' name were puzzling. The only deeds recorded in Miles' name were those for the purchase of 100 acres of land in 1815[13] and a subsequent sale of 100 acres in 1826,[14] but this time the deed listed

---

[13] Jesse Morgan to Miles Lassiter, Deed Book 13:402. FHLM #0019635 or #0470228.

[14] Sarah Lassiter and Miles Lassiter to Henry Newby, Deed Book 17:256. FHLM #0019636 or #0470229.

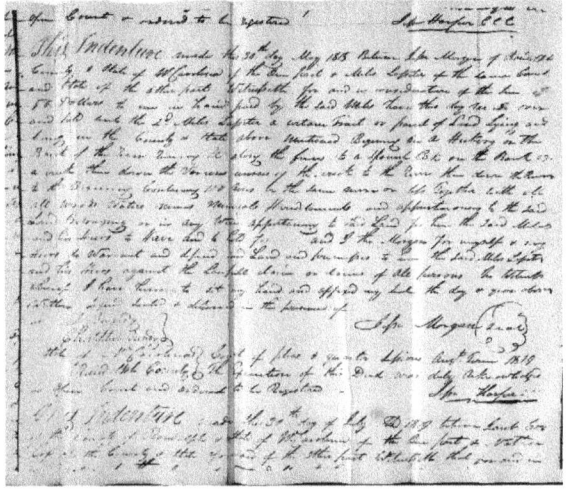

Figure 1.6: Miles' 1815 Deed

a Sarah Lassiter as well as Miles Lassiter as co-grantors. The only Sarah Lassiter of whom I was aware was the *Widow Lassiter*. She was reportedly the widow of Josiah Lassiter. She was a White woman who lived in the Lassiter Mill area of the county, southwest of Asheboro. She and her descendants were the only White Lassiter family in Randolph County. I suspected that the Widow Lassiter very likely had some relationship to Miles, but just what kind of relationship I didn't know. She and her husband may have been his owners at one time. On the other hand, I wondered if this could be a heretofore unknown woman named Sarah Lassiter, perhaps a woman of color, who even might have been the wife of Miles. Perhaps she had died before the 1850 census, which was the first census to list all the names of the individuals living in a household. While determining who she was and how she was related was intriguing, the more immediate question I had was, "If Miles sold his land in 1826, how is it the 1850 census showed that he owned real property worth about $590?"

Randolph County Historical Society

By this time I had done something that would later prove to be invaluable to me. I had contacted the Randolph County Library in Asheboro, and the Genealogical Society of Randolph County, which was headquartered at the library. I had found the name of the society in the resource section on North Carolina, in a genealogical 'how-to' book. I had become a member of the society, and was receiving their quarterly journal, a publication that makes a point of publishing original records from the county as well as queries from those doing research in the county. I had also called the library and spoken to one of the librarians, Carolyn Neely Hager. She was very knowledgeable about the county in general, and she said that the genealogical society was especially interested in learning more about the local African-American history. She also said they would be pleased to be of any assistance with my research, since they knew of only a few people actively researching the county's African American population.

Carolyn said that she knew some of the names I was researching, but suggested that I send an ancestor chart which would make it easier for her to sort out relationships and provide me with specific assistance. I sent her my charts and shortly thereafter she sent me a copy of a page from a book called *Farmer*,[15] on the Farmer community of greater Asheboro, where Lassiter Mill is located. The page referenced the Winston Lassiter family, including children Vella and Will Lassiter (presumably the same Will Lassiter to whom Ellen had sold her land). The page showed a picture of the family home, a red- brick, two-story house, with second-floor dormer windows and a large yard. More fortuitously yet, Carolyn had written across the top of the page that she believed this was my family, and that some of these people, specifically Vella Lassiter and

---

[15] Zeb R. Denny. *Farmer: Yesterday and Today* (Welcome, N.C.: Wooten Printing Co., Inc., 1981) 141.

Kate Lassiter Jones, still lived in the area. She also noted that Kate was particularly interested in local history. She suggested I get in touch, and provided addresses. I pulled out my printouts of the 1900 census, and noted Vella and Will's names. I was sure this was my family.

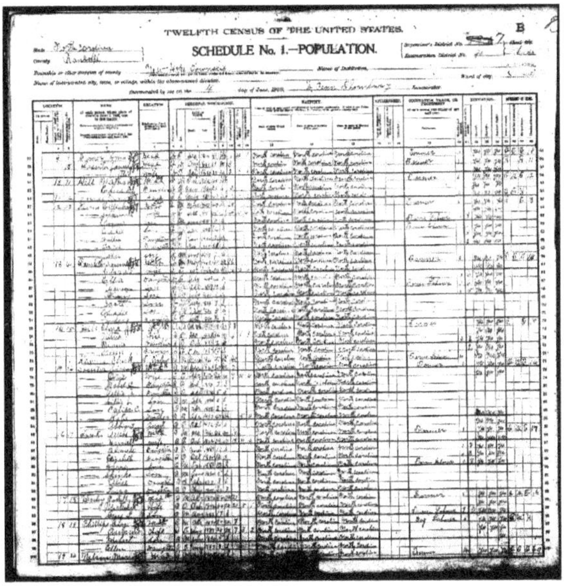
TWELFTH CENSUS OF THE UNITED STATES.

B

SCHEDULE No. 1.—POPULATION.

Figure 1.7: Lassiter Family 1900 from Ancestry.com

I was really excited and couldn't wait for the U.S. Post Office's snail mail, so I called information and obtained the phone number of Kate Jones. Her interest in county history gave me the perfect excuse for a phone call. I contacted her and explained that Carolyn Hager had suggested that I get in touch. She was very gracious. I told her that I was interested in the history of the African American presence in Randolph County. She spoke of her interest, and her desire, to one day write a book. After chatting some more about my parents, and saying that I hoped eventually to visit Randolph County (to which she graciously responded by saying I should visit her), I told her I had an even more personal reason for contacting her. I said, "Wasn't your grandfather Colier Lassiter?" to which she responded, "Yes." "Well," I said, "my great-great-great grandmother Nancy Lassiter was his sister." "What?" she exclaimed, "tell me that again." I repeated the relationship. "Well, my goodness," she said, "I didn't know that." I went on to explain about Grandma Ellen and her daughter, Louise. Kate told me that she was unfamiliar with those names; however, she said that her older sister, Vella, could probably tell me more. She encouraged me to make definite plans to visit, and, of course, to bring my mother.

Chapter 2

On the Road to Randolph County

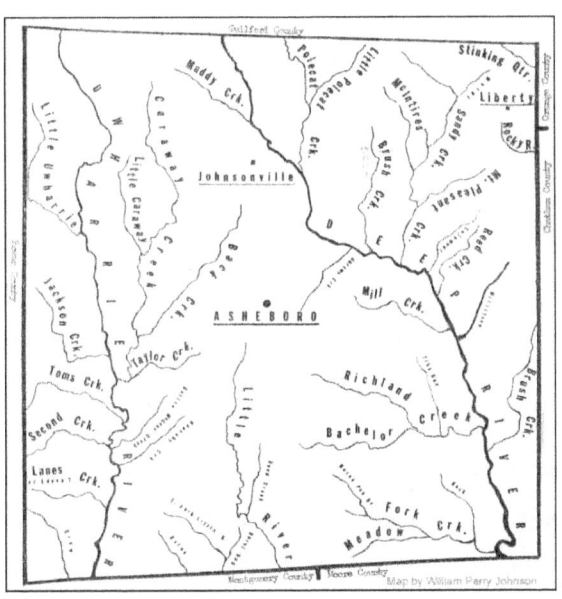

Figure 2.1: Randolph County NC Map

Randolph County Roots

Randolph County (county seat: Asheboro) is located in the Piedmont area of North Carolina, in what could be considered the geographical center of the state. It was formed in 1779, from the southern portion of Guilford County (county seat: Greensboro), which, in turn, was formed from Rowan and Orange Counties. There are three main rivers in Randolph: the Deep River which originates in Guilford County and runs southeastward to the Cape Fear River, which empties into the Atlantic Ocean; the Little River which arises near the center of the county and runs southward into the Pee Dee River which, in turn, runs through South Carolina before emptying into the Atlantic; and the Uwharrie, which originates in the Trinity area of the northwestern part of the county, runs southward past Lassiter's Mill in New Hope Township, then joins the Yadkin and finally into the Pee Dee. There are many creeks which empty into the Uwharrie. Those of importance for this story are primarily Back Creek, Hannah's Creek, Lane's Creek, Second Creek, and Walker's Creek.

Early reports by Europeans mention meetings with Sapona (Saponi) and Saura Indians, members of the Eastern Siouan cultures found in the Carolinas and Virginia. The writings of John Lawson, colonial Surveyor General of North Carolina mention the Keyauwee Indians (another of the Siouan tribes). Lawson noted that the land was fertile, with abundant wild-life, and the climate congenial, which he believed contributed to the large physical stature of the Keyauwee, and the presence among them of a significant number of older people, whom he described as *Gray-Heads*.[1]

Important to this area's accessibility for settlement by Europeans were the established Native American trading routes which ran north-south from the territory of the Cherokees and

---

[1] Barbara N. Grigg and Myrtle L. Walker, *Friends at Back Creek* (Greensboro: North Carolina Yearly Meeting of Friends, 1993), 13.

Catawbas, through the interior of the Carolinas, through Virginia, north into Pennsylvania, and New York, to the Iroquois territory. Four trading routes ran through what is today Randolph County. One road actually crossed the Uwharrie River at Lassiter's Mill.

Figure 2.2: Uwharrie River behind Lassiter's Mill

This was known as the Cape Fear-Salisbury (Rowan County seat) Road. Another road came down from Virginia, running along the east side of the Uwharrie River continuing on to South Carolina, and was called Moore's Road.[2] European-American settlers from New Jersey, Pennsylvania, Maryland and Virginia came to North Carolina (and Randolph County) along these roads. Many of today's roads follow these same routes.

---

[2] Ibid., 18.

The Drive South

In September 1982, my mother and I made our pilgrimage to Asheboro and Randolph County. It had been 62 years since my mother had been in North Carolina. She marveled out loud that it was her daughter who was taking her back. She also lamented that my dad, who had died in April, had not lived to make this trip—a trip he had often said he wanted to make.

We had mapped out our route. We would travel south on I-95, past Richmond, Virginia, then south of Petersburg, we would take I-85 through southwestern Virginia, across the North Carolina border. I-85 would take us past the exits for Raleigh, Durham, Chapel Hill, Hillsboro, and Burlington. Once arriving in the Greensboro area, we would look for, and exit onto State 220, headed south. Finally, not far from the business district of Asheboro, we would exit onto State 49, going south toward Charlotte. We were very excited as we drove to meet our cousins, wondering if we would be welcome, if we would have things in common, if all would be congenial. We even made contingency plans – if we did not feel comfortable, we would stay a couple of days (instead of the planned week), make our excuses, and drive out to Asheville, in the Great Smokies.

Once on 49, we were to look for the second crossroads, where we would turn right and then left onto what is now called Lassiter Mill Road. As we made the turns we passed Science Hill Friends Meeting. I recognized it from the book, *Farmer*. We were truly in the country as we rode along past farms and woodlands. We began to realize and be amused by the fact that we were now quite a few miles from the city of Asheboro, yet we knew that the postal address was still Asheboro.

Kate and the Family

We would drive along these quiet, rolling country roads for almost half an hour before realizing that we were coming to the

Figure 2.3: Lassiter Family home, Lassiter Mill Road, 1982

crossroads with what is now High Pine Church Road. As we approached the crossroads, I recognized a house to my left as being the one from the picture sent to me by Carolyn Hager, the one from the book, *Farmer*, the one where Vella and Will Lassiter lived. Driving around the corner onto High Pine Church Road, we were now approaching Kate Jones' home. As we drove up the driveway, Kate, her husband George (Ikie) Jones, and a couple of dogs greeted us. "Do we look related?" she asked with a big smile. Then, with hugs and kisses she ushered her new cousins into the house.

Actually, we did look related, especially my mom. How amazing to see people who looked like my mom after a lifetime of only seeing two people that looked like my mom: her sister Vern and me. Kate was a medium brown color, browner than my mother. Her face was oval rather than round like my mother's but it was the eyes that surprised me. They had the same shaped eyes. I later met Kate's brothers and sisters. They were varying shades of brown. Some were round-faced, others had longer, more oval-shaped faces, but they had the same shaped eyes.

Kate enthusiastically answered my questions telling me who married whom, the names of their children, and where they lived. While she didn't remember having ever heard of our

Figure 2.4: Margaret Lee Williams and Kate Lassiter Jones, 1982

family, or having met my mother, her brother Will claimed to have remembered my grandmother Elinora. However, they both knew many of the people and places my mother remembered, including Louise's sister Adelaide, Ellen's other daughter. Kate promised to take us to see these places, even to go up to Greensboro, in neighboring Guilford County, to visit the street where my mother had lived as a little girl before her mother died in the Flu epidemic of 1918, and before moving to New Jersey the first time.

The house there was next to A & T University, where from her yard during World War I, she could watch the Colored soldiers train. In addition, Kate invited many other cousins to come by the house to meet us. Again, while many of these relatives knew some of my mother's other cousins (most of whom, like Ellen, were now dead) they were unfamiliar with my mother.

Figure 2.5: Margaret Williams at A & T University, 1982

The Lassiter Mill Community

During our stay with Kate, she took us out to see the land. She drove us around the Lassiter Mill area (part of New Hope Township) along Lassiter Mill Road, pointing out the homes that had belonged to family members. She also drove us along High Pine Church Road, pointing out additional family homes, the fields which they farmed, and areas that they timbered. What I realized was that many of these homes were probably on the land that had been passed down to them by Colier Lassiter. Later, I asked Will where was the land he had received from my great great grandmother Ellen. He said it was across the road (Lassiter Mill Road), going toward the Uwharrie River. He said he kept cows on that land now. I was beginning to wish I had been able to be a part of this family during my growing up years. I realized I had missed something special, but I was grateful that I was now being embraced by my newly found cousins.

Naturally, I wanted to see the mill, Lassiter Mill. Our family had never owned the mill, but it had belonged to the White Lassiters. It was a major landmark in the community. It is on the Uwharrie River across the road that was named for the mill, *Lassiter Mill Road*. However the mill is actually more easily accessed from High Pine Church Road which intersects Lassiter Mill Road. Kate's husband Ikie took me across to see the mill. We walked there. He was carrying a shotgun, just in case we ran across any rattlesnakes.

The White Lassiters

What is known about the White Lassiters, the owners of the mill, has been published by several descendants, and I have both read some of those genealogies and spoken with some of the descendants that grew up in Randolph County. Published genealogical information about Josiah and Sarah Lassiter states that they came to the area around the mid 1760s, from eastern North Carolina, probably Gates County. When Josiah and Sarah came in the 1760s, Randolph County was still part of Rowan County. Descendants of this Lassiter couple have written that they acquired a large piece of property of 620 acres, in the southwestern quadrant of what had become Randolph County, in 1782. However, according to one descendant, Josiah died in 1778, making that purchase by him impossible. In addition, the purchase itself is not reflected in early deeds for Randolph County. Published lists of the Granville Land Grants (the earliest purchases of land from English Lord Granville during the colonial period) do not mention any Lassiters as purchasers of any land grants in Rowan or Orange Counties, the parent counties of Randolph County.³ So far, despite having examined records from Rowan County, Orange County, Guilford County (the immediate parent county of Randolph), and Randolph County for the time period, I have not been able to determine exactly when Josiah and Sarah came to what is now Randolph County.

Figure 2.6: Lassiter's Mill, 1982

Although establishing exactly when the Lassiters came to the area has been difficult, the presence of Sarah Lassiter and that of her son Micajah, as landowners in Randolph County has been well documented. Sarah Lassiter is listed in the first tax list for Randolph County, in 1779, when it was first created from Guilford County, as reported in *The Genealogical Journal* by The Randolph County Genealogical Society. The total value of all of her property is listed as 1440 Pounds.⁴ This abstraction did not mention specifically any land owned by Sarah. Sarah is listed on the 1785 tax list as having 200 acres on the "Uhary,"

---

³ Barbara N. Grigg, Carolyn N. Hager, and Francine H. Swaim, "Granville Land Grants," *The Genealogical Journal,* Randolph County Genealogical Society, Volume II, Number 2 (1978), 4.

⁴ "Randolph County's First Tax List, Part III," Ibid., Volume XXIV, Number 3 (2000), 36.

with one Black poll.[5] The 1799 tax list shows Sarah has only 90 acres, no White polls, but two Black polls, no mention of them being slaves.[6] In the same list, the only known son, Micajah Lassiter is listed as having 204 acres, with one White and one Black poll, again no mention of them being slaves.[7]

The earliest deed that I have discovered is one for a purchase by Sarah for 90 acres, in Randolph County in 1790, despite the 1785 tax listing for 200 acres. Repeated searches of the deed indexes for Rowan and Guilford Counties have turned up nothing prior to that date. Shortly after that, their only known son, Micajah Lassiter, bought over 500 acres. There were additional purchases in future years in Micajah's name. In 1811, Sarah sold her property to Ezekiel, "son of Micajah Lassiter," with rights to continue living in her home.[8] Although Micajah made other purchases, Sarah made no additional purchases. Nevertheless, she was a co-grantor with Miles Lassiter in 1826. I have not yet been able to substantiate when the Lassiters first purchased their farm.

Regardless of how or when they acquired their property, perhaps the most notable feature was that, in addition to farmland, there was a grist mill on their property. The mill was located along the west side of Uwharrie River, though it was moved in later years to the east side, where it still stands, tall and proud over the waters of the Uwharrie. It was and still is known as *Lassiter's Mill*, and can be reached from what is today called *High Pine Church Road*, near the intersection with Lassiter Mill Road. However, the mill is not currently in use. The mill lent its name to this community, which is called the Lassiter Mill community.

---

[5] "Randolph County Tax List–1785 (cont'd)," Ibid., 20.
[6] "Randolph County Tax List–1799," Ibid., Volume I, Number 1 (1977), 46.
[7] Ibid., 18.
[8] Sarah Lassiter to Ezekiel Lassiter, Deed Book 12:16. FHLM #19634.

Figure 2.7: Strieby Congregational UCC Church, 1982

Church and Family

Kate also drove us out to Strieby, in neighboring Union Township, where Strieby Congregational United Church of Christ Church and Cemetery are located. Here she showed us where one of the first African American churches had been built, and where their school had once stood. The church was founded by the Rev. Islay Walden, a former Smitherman slave who became a missionary of the American Missionary Association. Today he is considered one of the 100 best African-American poets who ever lived. She showed us the graves of those who had gone before, including her parents Winston and Ora, and Abigail, Colier and Nancy's sister (who lived to be 110 years old), and the graves of many other family members.

In this area, on lands surrounding the church, lived cousins who were also a part of the large Hill clan that lent its name to the area. It was once referred to as *Hill Town*, since so many of the Hill family members lived there. My mother had heard of Hill Town, and even heard of Strieby. Later, she told me that her grandmother Louise occasionally went there when they were living in Asheboro, but she had never been there. When

Figure 2.8: Strieby Church Cemetery, 1982

her grandmother went there, she and her sister would stay with Aunt Ammy and Uncle George (Amma and George Phillips), Louise's younger sister and husband, who lived in Asheboro.

Kate drove us over to the Mechanic area in Cedar Grove township, where another of our family's clans had settled—the Birkheads and Crosses. Here and further down Highway 49, were St. Mark United Methodist Church and Salem Congregational United Church of Christ. Each of these churches had cemeteries where additional family members had been buried, including Ellen's sister Adelaide, her husband Solomon Kearns, and their daughters. Near St. Mark's there had also been another well-known one room school house for African Americans, *Red House School*. Family members, including Vella Lassiter, had been teachers both here and at Strieby.

Kate also drove us to Asheboro, to what was the Old Plank Road, now North Fayetteville St., where Grandma Ellen's house once stood. It's a busy, primarily commercial part of town now. We also drove around to Salisbury St., where my mother lived for a time with her grandmother Louise, after Grandma Ellen died in 1920. We thought we had identified the house, but learned later that her house was a couple of

Figure 2.9: Home of Arthur Hill, Strieby, NC, 1982

doors away, and had been replaced by the telephone company's offices. We also saw where Louise's younger sister Amma, her husband George Phillips, and their children lived and ran a dinner club. It is now St. Sardis Church. We also saw the First Congregational Church, where my mother remembered attending Sunday School.

I was curious about the family's church affiliations. I had already learned by looking in the *Encyclopedia of Quaker Genealogy* that Miles had requested to become a Quaker in 1845.[9] I inquired about this. Kate and Vella and the others said that they did not know if Miles was a Quaker, but they knew that his son, Colier, had been a Quaker, and that he was buried in the Quaker cemetery at Uwharrie. I asked why the rest of the family had not followed the Quaker tradition. No one seemed to know why, just that they hadn't. Still they affirmed the strong relationship Quakers had with the community, and the help they had provided to slaves and free people of color. I still did not know at that time that Miles was not only a Quaker, but one of

---

[9] William Wade Hinshaw, *Encyclopedia of Quaker Genealogy, 1750-1930* (Baltimore: Genealogical Publishing Company) Back Creek Monthly Meeting, I:723.

Figure 2.10: Margaret Williams on Old Salisbury St., 1982

very few African American Quakers in North Carolina, and the only one at the time of his death. I would learn about that later.

I was feeling as though I had made a pilgrimage, an ancestral pilgrimage. This place, this land was my home. My roots were here. My ancestors were here. Miles was here. I began to understand that the land was, in many ways, the glue that had held this family together, and it undoubtedly held the secrets to our family's history. I was going to have to follow the land if I was going to unravel the various family relationships and history—including how my mother and her sister had become isolated and estranged from this family and this land.

Figure 2.11: St. Sardis

Figure 2.12: First Congregational Church, 1982

Chapter 3

Tracing the Land

Figure 3.1: Ellen Dunson Smitherman Mayo land

Hildy

While in Asheboro, I went to the county library and met Carolyn Hager. Carolyn showed me the few files they had on African

Americans in the county, how to use their microfilmed records, and a file on the White Lassiter family, including the widow Sarah Lassiter. In this file I located the only other reference to land owned by my Lassiter family in a short, undocumented family history kept in the Lassiter folder. It stated that there was an oral tradition in the family that 409 acres had been given to a Mrs. Benjamin H. Lassiter and a Mrs. Andrews upon their freedom, and that the lands were still in the possession of descendants.[1]

Who were these women? Was Mrs. Lassiter Miles' mother? Was Mrs. Andrews a sister? No documents I had identified or examined to this point, including deeds and probate records, had provided any supporting evidence for who these women might have been. I checked with Kate and other family members. They were unfamiliar with these names. However, Harold Lassiter, Kate's youngest brother, said he remembered that Miles' wife's name was Hildy.

Estate of Healy Phillips or Lassiter

The first real clue to the property came after I returned home to Maryland. I received a new issue of *The Genealogical Journal* by the Randolph County Genealogical Society that published an abstract of the intestate probate record of "Healy Phillips or Lassiter." It named Colier, Abigail, Wiley, Nancy, Jane, Susannah, and Emsley Phillips or Lassiter as heirs at law.[2] Except for Emsley and Susannah, I had seen all of these names in Miles' household on the 1850 census, and an Emsley was included in Nancy and Calvin Dunson's household in 1860, but no Susannah was mentioned. This probate, recorded in Will Book 10, distributed a home tract and mountain tract to the heirs. Curi-

---

[1] J. HA. Lassiter, *Lassiter Genealogy*, dated 10/18/1950, as copied by Ray Riechley in 1965.

[2] "Phillips Heirs," *The Genealogical Journal,* the Randolph County Genealogical Society, VI (Winter 1982): 51-52.

ously, the probate was undated. I decided to look in the Will Books myself, as well as the court minutes.

I went to the Family History Center and ordered microfilmed copies of the Will Books that held the probate records, and copies of the microfilmed minutes of the Court of Common Pleas and Quarter Sessions. There were not many references either to Miles or Healy, but there were some important and interesting discoveries:

- Will Book 10 covered the years 1853-56, with Healy's probate listed among 1854/55 probates;

- There were no accompanying letters of administration recorded in the Will Book; and

- The probate was not referenced in the minutes of the Court of Common Pleas and Quarter Sessions as it should have been.

Thus, Healy's estate probably wasn't probated until about 1854, but she seemed to have died before 1850. Perhaps this was closer to when Miles had died. It was even more strange to note that there were no letters of administration, nor any recording of the probate in the court minutes.

The distribution to the heirs at law, as recorded in Will Book 10, included a home tract and mountain tract valued at $755. The final total of the entire estate after appropriate and necessary deductions was $802.19. However, no physical description of the property was given in this probate. At least some land belonging to descendants may have originated with "Healy Phillips or Lassiter." This was reasonably consistent with the tradition, mentioned above, among the heirs of the Widow Sarah Lassiter.

So, who was this "Healy Phillips or Lassiter"? The 1840 census showed a Heley Phillips[3] as head of household with age

---
[3] As was common in this time period, spelling was not standardized, both

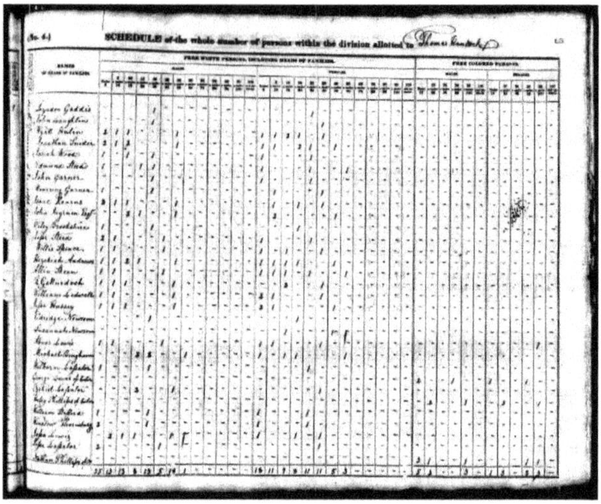

Figure 3.2: Heley Phillips 1840 census

and gender distributions of household members comparable to the 1850 census of Miles, but with the important addition of a female in the same age category as Miles.[4] This seemed consistent with what I had learned from Harold Lassiter.[5] I sought additional information about her, but few other records from the time period mentioned her name. I had seen her name in this census before. I had seen it while researching my Sam Phillips' family. Sam was my mother's grandfather, husband of Mama Louise. At that time, I thought perhaps Healy was related to him. In fact, I thought Healy was the male head of household in the 1840 census, not a female. I had not had any reason until now to think that there was a connection to Miles.

---

spellings *Healy* and *Heley* are found interchangeably. This paper uses the now standardized spelling *Healy* as the norm.

[4] 1840 US Census, Randolph County, North Carolina, Heley Phillips, p. 65. NAM #M704-369.

[5] Per a conversation with Harold Cleon Lassiter, great grandson of Miles Lassiter, in September 1982.

Tracing the Land

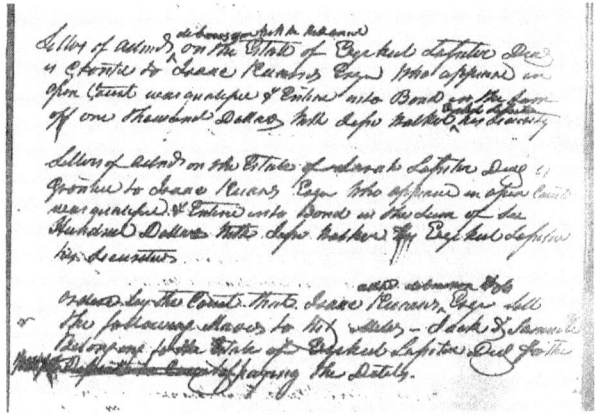

Figure 3.3: Ezekiel Lassiter Letters of Administration

Other Records

In order to search for any information about Healy, the land, Miles, and their relationship to one another in that time period, I needed to search as many different types of records as possible. Included in that search were all early land records of the White Lassiters, all court minutes from the time period, and all probate records for the Lassiters.

In the minutes of the Court of Common Pleas and Quarter Sessions, I found:

- An 1807 order for Miles, Jack and Samuel Lassiter to assist with maintenance of the Fayetteville Road.[6]

- An 1818 bastardy bond for Heleah Phelps, no male mentioned.[7]

In the Will Books, I found probate information for Sarah Lassiter and an Ezekiel Lassiter. I wondered if this was her

---

[6] Road maintenance assignment, 1807 Minutes of the Court of Common Pleas and Quarter Sessions. FHLM #0470210.

[7] Heleah Phelps, Bastardy Bond, Minutes of the Court of Common Pleas and Quarter Sessions, February 1818. FHLM #0470210.

grandson. In any event, this Ezekiel's estate was being probated in 1840 along with Sarah's. Ezekiel's probate had information about Miles, Jack and Samuel. They were listed as slaves, and they were being sold. Thus, there was:

- The February 1840 purchase for $0.05 of Miles by Heley Phillips "col'd," Jack for $12.50 by "Colier, coul'd man," and in April, Samuel who was in jail, by Sawney Cranford for $262.25;[8]

and in the Deed Books, I found:

- An 1842 listing as a trustee under the name Healy Lassiter for a deed of trust with Edward Hill.[9]

This deed was the first real clue that Miles and Healy might be husband and wife.

Miles and Healy, Husband and Wife

According to court minutes noted above, Healy had a child out of wedlock... or did she? After all, since marriage for a slave (Miles) would be illegal, there would be no point in naming him because he would have no legal standing and not be able to post a bond. Perhaps this referred to another man. There were no clues. However, I still wasn't convinced that I had accurate information about whether Healy was Miles' wife or not. I wanted more proof.

As cited previously, Healy purchased Miles for the sum of five cents from the Lassiter estate. This suggested that it was largely a symbolic purchase, probably because of his advanced

---

[8] Estate of Ezekiel Lassiter, Will Book 7:332. FHLM #0019643.
[9] Edward Hill to Samuel Hill, Ezekiel Lassiter, et al., Deed Book 25:1, FHLM #0019639 or #0470232.

age and crippled condition. If he was her husband, it would have been appropriate for her to purchase him.[10]

What finally convinced me (at this point in my research) that she was indeed Miles' wife was finding her name *Healy Lassiter*, listed as a trustee *(how could she do that?)* for someone else's property, Edward (Ned) Hill. He was the patriarch of the Hill clan.[11] This reference to her as a Lassiter indicated she chose to be known by her married name, now that Miles was possibly freed by her.

I actually found this record quite by accident. Her name was not listed in the index, but was subsumed in the term "et al." Because I was trying to learn as much about Lassiter land purchases as possible in an effort to find how Miles' family acquired their land, I was reading all Lassiter deeds, including all those of the White Lassiters. If I had not been doing this, I would have missed this record.

In an attempt to unravel this mystery, I wrote to the Friends Historical Collection at Guilford College where I was told there were probably records of Back Creek Meeting, the Friends Meeting where Miles has been accepted into membership in 1845. I hoped that there might be some mention of Healy, possibly even her date of death, or some confirmation of her marriage to Miles, and possibly the exact date of death for Miles. They responded that although there was information about Miles, there was no mention of Healy, no marriage date, and no death date for Miles. They did note that he disappeared from the records in 1850 and probably died after that.[12] So there was nothing to be learned about his marriage or death.

---

[10] Ed. note: This was not uncommon. For example, Martin Delaney's freeborn mother purchased her husband (Delaney's father) upon migrating the family to Pittsburgh in 1822.

[11] Edward Hill to Samuel Hill, Ezekiel Lassiter, et al., Deed Book 25:1, FHLM #0019639 or #0470232.

[12] Treadway letter, 30 October 1987.

Chapter 4

Life in Pre-Civil War Randolph County

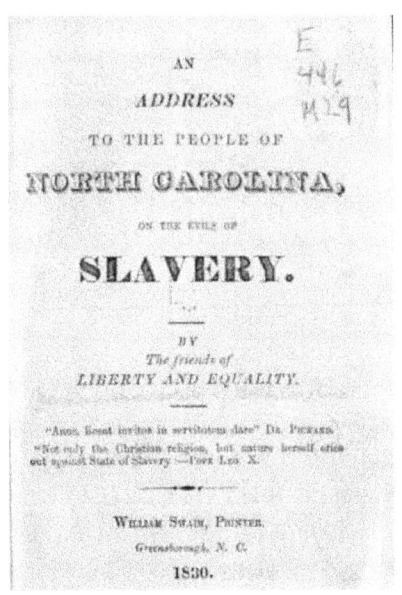

Figure 4.1: North Carolina Manumission Society Flyer

Slave or Free

In the last chapter I noted that in 1807, Miles, Jack, and Samuel were ordered by the court to assist Micajah Hill as overseers of the Fayetteville Road. That seemed to indicate that they were free. That, in turn, seemed to be consistent with the 1830 census, which listed Miles as a free head of household. On the other hand, he was named as a slave in the 1840 probate of Ezekiel Lassiter's estate. I was puzzled. *Which was he, slave or free?*

The Lassiter Slaves

The Lassiters apparently had only a handful of slaves. Miles should have been one of them in 1778, when Josiah supposedly died. Therefore, Miles would have been one of the five slaves recorded in the 1790 census belonging to Sarah Lassiter.[1] Two of the others were probably his brothers, Jack and Samuel. I had no reliable information about the remaining two. At least one descendant of Sarah's wrote in a family history that these two other slaves were a Mrs. Benjamin Lassiter, and a Mrs. Andrews. Other than the mention of these two women in this context, I have been unable to find anything which refers to them, and none of Miles' descendants that I have contacted has any knowledge of them.

Miles' life as a slave appears to have been one of unusual privilege. In fact, his status as a slave has been a puzzle. Although descendants of Sarah Lassiter say that he was given his freedom in the 1780s or 90s, efforts to find documentation of this have proved futile. The earliest known primary record pertaining to Miles and his brothers that I have been able to locate was the 1807 Fayetteville Road maintenance order.[2] This was interesting because, as a rule, only free people would be named

---

[1] 1790 U.S. Census, Randolph County, North Carolina, Sarah Lassiter, 100. NAM #T498-2, item 2.
[2] Road Orders, August 1807. FHLM #0019650 or #0470209.

by the courts to road maintenance. Slaves would simply be sent by their owners, who might themselves have been named to the road maintenance. There was no mention in this record that Miles and his brothers were slaves. Even more interesting, neither Miles nor his brothers were even referenced as being persons of color in this record. Miles was even listed in the 1830 census, as a *free* head of household (the 1820 census no longer exists for this county).[3] Based on this information, I assumed that the tradition that he had been freed was accurate. The only mention of Miles and his brothers as slaves was in the 1840 inventory and final distribution of the estate of Ezekiel Lassiter. I had concluded that some political misfortunes had prompted Sarah and her family to become Miles' owner of record in order to protect him, especially since the late 1820s and 1830s saw the enactment of increasingly restrictive laws regarding free people of color, the so-called Black Codes.

As noted, descendants of Sarah Lassiter had said that Miles had been freed by her in the 1790s. That seemed to be supported by the1807 road crew record, the 1830 census, and his purchases of land. On the other hand, there was the 1840 probate. I wondered what laws, including the Black Codes, might shed light on this seeming contradiction.

Black Codes and Randolph County

Randolph County in the late 18th to early 19th century was rural, with primarily family farms and small merchants owning relatively few slaves. In 1850, only 14 percent of 2,527 households owned slaves in Randolph County.[4] This was not a com-

---

[3] 1830 US Census, Randolph County, North Carolina, Miles Lassiter, p. 7. NAM #M19-125.

[4] Charles L. Gray, Sr., *Gray and Watkins Family History, Randolph County and Guilford County*: Volume I, *The Gray/Watkins Family History* (Temple Hills, MD: Charles L. Gray, 2002), 11. These statistics were taken from: *Randolph County, 1779-1979* (Winston-Salem, NC: Hunter Publishing Company, 1979), 72.

munity of large plantations based on extensive slave labor, like the tobacco plantations of eastern North Carolina, or the rice plantations of South Carolina. There were a few large farms that relied more heavily on slave labor, but they were not the norm. Five farms owned between 20 and 30 slaves, and one owned 39. General Alexander Gray was the largest slave-owner with 119 slaves. Others owned fewer than 20, and 117 owned only one.[5] Randolph County did not have many slave traders either. This meant that the slave population was relatively stable, with close relationships between slave owners and slaves. This was not atypical in North Carolina. John Hope Franklin wrote in his book, *The Free Negro in North Carolina, 1790-1860*, that in 1860, 67 percent of slaveholders had fewer than 10 slaves, and 72 percent of the population had no slaves at all. He stated that, "The farm labor in North Carolina was done not only by the slaves but, in some areas, by White farming families, White farm laborers, as well as free Negro farm laborers."[6] This, he speculated, led to close relationships, thereby fostering tolerance which, in turn, led to a lack of strict enforcement of Black Codes with regard to slavery.

Randolph County also developed a sizeable free non-White population. In 1850, there were 397 free people of color, or 24 percent of the population.[7] Again, this was not unusual for North Carolina. In 1790, there were 5,041 free people of color in North Carolina. By 1860, there were 30,463.[8] A significant portion of the free population of color was biracial and tri-racial, mixed African/Native American/European individuals. Many of these were children of free mothers (White and non-White), who were therefore free by law, but those whose mothers were slaves, were themselves consigned to slavery. However, it was not unknown for White fathers to set their children free. Added to this environment was the presence of a large number of abo-

---

[5] Ibid.
[6] John Hope Franklin, *The Free Negro in North Carolina, 1790-1860*, 147.
[7] Op. Cit.
[8] Ibid., 18.

litionists in North Carolina. Members of the Society of Friends, known as Quakers, who were committed abolitionists, as well as Presbyterian, Methodist, and Moravian abolitionists, both supported and protected the free community. The Quaker practice of buying up slaves and then setting them free became so frequent that in 1827 the North Carolina State Supreme Court attempted to stop them by ruling that Quakers could no longer hold slaves.[9] This did not stop them from continuing to help slaves gain their freedom. Randolph County was considered a Quaker stronghold, and Quaker efforts to free slaves and protect free people of color are still recounted. Despite these efforts to protect free people of color, they were frequently subject to kidnapping and sale. If they were lucky, they had recourse to the courts to help them regain their freedom, but there were those who never did regain freedom.

At the turn of the 19th century, there was an increase in manumissions for meritorious service in North Carolina. This was largely the result of the growing manumission movement. Quakers organized the North Carolina Manumission Society, which was prominent in Randolph, Guilford, and Rowan counties. By 1826, there were 23 branches with more than a thousand members in six counties including Randolph and Guilford Counties. Between 1824 and 1826, the society freed more than 2000 slaves in North Carolina.[10] By 1830, the manumission laws were generally being ignored. The North Carolina General Assembly tried to strengthen the laws regarding manumission, but they continued to be ignored in many areas. On the other hand, it continued to be lawful for someone to free their slaves in their last will and testament, or to free any slave over fifty years old for meritorious service. Thus, slave owners continued to free their slaves by a variety of means, both legal and not legal.[11] In addition, those who were free also worked to purchase

---

[9] Ibid., 24.
[10] Ibid., 26.
[11] Ibid., 27.

the freedom of relatives and friends.[12]

Education and Religion

There were no government sponsored social welfare programs in the early 19th century, other than poor houses. In the late 18th and early 19th centuries, concerns that free children of color, *base-born* children (born out of wedlock), regardless of color, and those whose parents could not care for them led to laws requiring these children to be apprenticed in order to learn farming skills or to learn a trade. This was not so much a concern for the welfare of these children as much as it was a concern that these children should not become vagrants, and thus a burden on the community.

Many of the free children of color were bound to other free tradesmen of color.[13] In the early years, these children were bound until they were 16 years of age. Part of their training was being taught to read and write. By 1838, the master of a free apprentice of color was no longer required to teach him/her to read and write, however, many continued to do so. In 1851, the master was forbidden to take his apprentices out of the county. There were discrepancies, however, in the length of service required for White apprentices and those of color. White female apprentices could be released from service at age 18, while apprentices of color were required to serve until age 21. Still, apprenticeships were one of the most successful means for educating free people of color in terms of both vocational training and literacy.[14] Franklin reported that Randolph County had 49 apprentices in 1860.[15] It is noteworthy that no record has been discovered that refers to any of Miles and Healy's children having been apprenticed.

---

[12] Ibid., 29.
[13] Ibid., 123-126.
[14] Ibid., 129.
[15] Ibid., 227.

In addition to apprenticeship training, there were some schools set up for free people of color. Again, Quakers were particularly active in this area. They reportedly began teaching slaves as early as 1771. In Randolph County, in the 1850 census, there were reportedly 6 free people of color who were in school.[16] In considering the implications of literacy for free people across the state, Franklin explained that one could speculate that in addition to those in school, there were many more at home being quietly, even secretly taught to read and write. He reported that for the whole state of North Carolina in 1850, there were 12,048 free adults of color, and 5191, or 43 percent, reported some degree of literacy.[17]

In many ways literacy was dependent on religion. Most educational efforts among people of color, whether slave or free, African, Native, or mixed, were made by religious groups, with individual ministers frequently being the teachers. Perhaps one of the best known ministers and educators of the time was himself a free person of color, John Chavis. Among the various White religious denominations that attempted to provide some education, Anglicans (Episcopalians) began their educational efforts as early as 1763, through the Society for the Propagation of the Gospel. Presbyterians, Methodists, and Quakers were also active.[18]

Still, there were few actual religious opportunities specifically for people of color, whether slave or free. There were no Black-run churches in North Carolina in the late 18th century. Frequently they were seated in special sections during regular services at the White churches, or had special services at the end of the regular services.[19] There were some free people of color who were preachers/ministers in this period, most notably John Chavis, the Presbyterian minister and teacher mentioned above, and Ralph Freeman, who was a Baptist minister and mis-

---

[16] Ibid., 169n.
[17] Ibid., 151.
[18] Ibid., 165-66.
[19] Ibid., 170.

sionary whose route included Randolph County. Unfortunately, the law of 1831 which forbade active preaching by all preachers and ministers of color, whether free or slave, effectively ended these Black ministries.[20]

Quakers and Back Creek Friends Meeting

Among White denominations, the members of the Society of Friends (Quakers) were well-known for their efforts to abolish slavery, including their participation in the Underground Railroad as *Conductors*. Their abolitionist history is an important part of North Carolina history and Randolph County was home to a large Quaker community.

Quakers came to North Carolina as early as 1660, settling primarily in the area of Albemarle Sound, in the counties of Perquimans and Pasquotank. They began moving west in search of new land and to escape the mosquito borne tropical diseases prevalent along the coast. They settled in areas of what was then Orange and Rowan Counties, but later divided into Alamance, Chatham, Guilford, and Randolph Counties.[21]

Back Creek Meeting is the oldest Quaker meeting in Randolph County. Beginning in 1785, Friends living in the Back Creek area of Randolph County (named for a creek that empties into the Uwharrie River) petitioned to become an official monthly meeting. Their first meeting house was built in 1789. After evaluation by the quarterly meeting at Cane Creek (Rowan County), Back Creek held its first monthly meeting 12 November 1792. In 1820, a quarterly meeting was begun at Back Creek.[22]

Back Creek Friends community was also interested in education. In 1831, a committee was appointed to oversee the organization of a school. By 1835, the committee seemed to

---

[20] Ibid., 180.
[21] *Friends at Back Creek*, 23.
[22] Ibid., 24-28.

feel that the primary need was for a Sabbath Day School (aka Sunday School). Back Creek is thought to have established the first Sunday School in the area. The school met in the summer. At first it was only for youth, but soon involved all ages. The only text book was the Bible. Back Creek finally opened an academic school after the Civil War.[23]

It is interesting to note that despite their extensive work among slaves, Quakers seemed reluctant to admit people of color to their meetings. The case of Isaac Linegar of Guilford County is a well-known example. In 1798, he requested membership in the Deep River Monthly Meeting. The case was referred to the New Garden Quarterly Meeting, and then the North Carolina Yearly Meeting and continued for over two years before finally being resolved and Linegar was admitted on 6 June 1801. Although John Hope Franklin speculated that others must have followed suit, there is no real evidence that this happened.[24] Henry Cadbury in his article in the *Journal of Negro History*, "Negro Membership in the Society of Friends," said there was little evidence of formal membership, although there was evidence that slaves transferred to their care, or freed, continued to attend meetings.[25] One of the few documented North Carolina cases of official membership to which Cadbury referred, was that of Miles Lassiter, reportedly the only African American Quaker in North Carolina at the time of his death in 1850.[26]

Property

The purchase, sale, or other ownership of property involves contracts. As such slaves were unable to make legal contracts since

---

[23] Ibid., 31-32.

[24] Franklin, 175.

[25] Henry Cadbury, "Negro Membership in the Society of Friends" (Part 1), *Journal of Negro History*, 21, 151-213. (1936), This Document is on <http://www.qhpress.org/quakerpages/qwhp/qwhp.htm>.

[26] Ibid., Part 3.

they had no legal standing. Free people of color, on the other hand, were able to purchase, own, and sell land. That right was continually upheld by the courts. Free people were also able to distribute their land to their heirs by means of wills. When there were no wills the courts distributed their property in accordance with the laws that governed intestate (no will) probates.[27] It is just this legal inconsistency that has led to confusion over Miles' status.

While the law allowed free people to acquire property, actually doing so was difficult, since the vast majority of free people were relatively poor. There were a few who were able to amass sizeable estates, but most property owners had property worth only a few hundred dollars and most free people owned no property. In Randolph County, in 1860, there were between 300 and 500 free people of color, according to the census information reported by Franklin.[28] By contrast, Franklin identified no free people in Randolph County in the same time period who owned property worth $2500 or more, but he did report that there were 14 real property owners, (of which 7 were farmers, including Miles' son, Colier Lassiter) and 65 personal property owners.[29]

As mentioned previously, free people of color sometimes owned slaves. Frequently these slaves were their family members, but some owned slaves as laborers. The right to own slaves was also upheld by the courts. In 1833, the North Carolina Supreme Court ruled that free people of color could own land and property, including slaves. Some had questioned whether free people of color were in fact full citizens, since the law had treated them in other instances as a special class of citizen with special laws enacted regulating their lives (such as apprenticeships, or slave/free marriages). The court ruled that they were citizens within the full meaning of the law with regard to the

---

[27] Ibid., 150-155.
[28] Franklin, 175.
[29] Cadbury, 228-232. Ancestry.com's index of the 1860 census, published in 2006 on the world-wide web, showed 296 individuals listed as *Mulatto*, and 162 as *Black*, for a total of 458 free people of color in Randolph County.

ownership of property, including slave property. This ruling remained in effect until 1860-61, when the Civil War began. At that time, the General Assembly passed legislation preventing free people from buying, owning, hiring, or otherwise having control over slaves, but the legislation exempted those who already possessed slaves.[30] With regard to Miles, there is no way of knowing why Healy did not buy Miles' freedom sooner, or simply buy him as her property prior to 1840.

Marriage between slaves and free people

Slave marriages were not legally recognized in English-speaking North America. Since slaves were property and not persons, they had no legal standing to contract a marriage. On the other hand, free people of color were legally able to marry, and many made the appropriate applications and posted the necessary bonds in order to achieve that legal standing. Their records can be found in the courthouse records along with those of White residents in the counties where they lived.

However, there was another category of marriage which the state regulated—marriages between free persons and slaves. In 1787, the North Carolina General Assembly passed a law that required free people who intended to marry a slave to get the written permission of the slave owner, or they would be fined.[31] Nevertheless, many free people continued to marry slaves, with no evidence of written permission. In 1830, in the wake of increased concerns over slave uprisings, the General Assembly made it against the law for free people of color to marry slaves. Franklin speculated that this 1830 marriage law, like the 1787 law, was not very strictly followed and free people continued to marry slaves.[32] Such relationships provided a possible avenue

---
[30] Ibid., 156.
[31] Franklin, 184.
[32] John Hope Franklin, *The Free Negro in North Carolina, 1790-1860*, 184-85.

to freedom, since the free person could potentially purchase the freedom of the slave spouse. However, there is no evidence that this was a significant path of manumission.

No record of a marriage for Miles and Healy has been located, but the absence of a record does not mean he was not free. No evidence of permission to marry has been identified either. Again, it may not have survived. Nevertheless, for at least a portion of their married life Miles was a slave and Healy was free. This was confirmed in a letter written by Jonathan Worth in 1851, after both Miles and Healy were dead.

Restrictions

In general the relationships between slaves and free people of color became increasingly restricted by legal enactments. In particular, the laws passed between 1826 and 1830 restricted both social and economic activities. Free people of color found their world becoming narrower and narrower.[33] Though some have speculated that these codes were a result of the Nat Turner Rebellion in Virginia, Franklin pointed out that most of these laws were already in place over a year before the rebellion.[34] Interestingly enough, the right of free people of color to bear arms was not restricted until 1840, and even slaves could bear arms if their owners gave them permission and posted bond attesting to their good behavior. Another interesting restriction prevented slaves from acting as though they were free, but Franklin did not provide any details.[35] Politically, free people of color had been able to vote in North Carolina since 1734, but legislation was passed in 1835, after much debate, and a close vote, that disenfranchised them.[36]

This was North Carolina, including Randolph County, in

---

[33] Ibid., 184-189.
[34] Ibid., 70-72, see especially note 68, on page 72.
[35] Ibid., 72.
[36] Ibid., 105-120.

the late 18th and early 19th centuries. This was the world Miles Lassiter and his family knew.

Chapter 5

The People on the Land

Figure 5.1: Descendants of Miles and Healy Lassiter

The Heirs of Healy Phillips

Healy's probate record did not provide the information I sought on the actual division of the lands mentioned, nor any other lands, into distinct parcels to specific heirs. It did not even provide a precise death date. Thus, while the probate record provided clues to the ownership of the land and to the relationship of Healy to the others (remembering that an inheritance generally passes first to spouse, children, and/or grandchildren before parents, siblings, or others) it also raised a number of interesting questions.

Since Healy was not listed in the 1850 census, I assumed that she actually died between the 1840 and 1850 censuses, and based on the 1842 deed of trust with Ned Hill, between 1842 and 1850. So why wasn't Miles listed as an heir? As mentioned, "Will Book 10" covered the years 1853-1856. If it was true that Miles died about 1850, it seemed that the estate was not probated until after his death. If not, why not? I can only assume that no one saw a need to pursue the probate process until Miles died. I had noticed that beginning in 1851 a deed for land of nearly 400 acres began to appear in Colier's name. This seemed to support the theory that this was the time Miles had died. Examination of this deed indicated that Nancy, Wiley, Susannah, and Emsley (via an attorney—did that mean he was a minor?), in a deed dated 28 June 1851, sold their rights to the land to Colier.[1] That tract was described as being adjacent to the properties of Josiah T. Lassiter and Barnabas Boswell. Even though this deed was dated 1851, it was not recorded until 1855. It may be that because this sale was apparently between family members, they did not feel a need to go to the courthouse to have it proved and recorded. However, in 1855, Colier sought a deed of trust on three hundred acres of the property, and was probably required to prove ownership.[2] With that, I assumed that an assessment of the property was made and an accounting and final distribution recorded in Will Book 10. The deed of trust to Samuel Hill (who had been the attorney of record for Ems-

---

[1] Emsley and Susan Lassiter, et al, to Calier Phillips, Deed Book 29:495. FHLM #0470233.

[2] Colier Lassiter to Samuel Hill (Tr), Deed Book 30:15, FHLM #0470234.

ley) was then properly recorded in both the Deed Books and the minutes of the Court of Common Pleas and Quarter Sessions, as was the 1851 transaction between Colier and the others.[3] It didn't make sense. If Nancy, mother of Ellen, had relinquished all claim to these lands, then what land was divided and apportioned to Ellen? Also, in what record was this division noted? Finally, there still remained the question of where the land had come from. How and when did the family first acquire it?

The Genealogical Journal

A new clue to the land was found when I read a published article in an issue of *The Genealogical Journal* by the Randolph County Genealogical Society, which I was receiving regularly. Sometime before 1857, the 100-acre tract of land bought from Jesse Morgan and sold to Henry Newby seemed to have found its way back into the hands of the Lassiter family. In that year, Thomas Newby, one of Henry's sons who had moved to Indiana, probably with the Quaker migration, was visiting in the area. He wrote in a diary, published by *The Genealogical Journal*, that he stopped for dinner at the home of Calvin Lassiter, "where father used to live."[4] (*Calvin* Lassiter was a spelling occasionally found in the records for *Colier* Lassiter, Miles' son, probably from misreading an alternative spelling *Calier*.) Thomas Newby's visit would not have been unusual since Colier was considered a Quaker, who attended meeting regularly, although no record of his admission to a meeting has been located. Herein may lie the secret, I thought. Newby, Miles, and Colier were fellow Quakers. It would not be unusual, when moving west to Indiana, that Newby might have considered returning (or even

---

[3] Recording of deeds: Emsley and Susan Lassiter, et al. and Calier Phillips (Deed 29:495); and Colier Lassiter to Samuel Hill (Deed 30:15), February 1855, Court of Common Pleas and Quarter Sessions. FHLM #0470212 or #0019653.

[4] "Thomas Newby Diary, Part VII," *The Genealogical Journal* by the Randolph County Genealogical Society, V, 4 (Fall 1981): 29-30.

selling back) the land he had bought from Miles, to Colier. *What about the rest of the land? Where did it come from?*

In a subsequent issue of *The Genealogical Journal* by the Randolph County Genealogical Society, an article about Wiley Lassiter was published. It was a petition, and in it Wiley (called Willie) notes that he had acquired two tracks of property about five or six years prior—one tract of 275 acres, the other 155 acres.[5] This seemed to refer to the inheritance of the land after both Healy and Miles had died. Still the question I had was, *Where did she get the land?*

The County Library

I made several trips to Lassiter Mill in the years after my first pilgrimage. I usually tried to make at least one side trip into Asheboro, to the county library, checking for any new information that might have become available. On one of these trips, around 1986, I made one of my most meaningful discoveries. In the folder on African Americans was a newspaper clipping from an article about a memorial plaque in the Old City Cemetery. One of the names shown on the plaque was that of my great-great-great grandmother Nancy Dunson. The plaque itself was dedicated to various people of color, all contemporary to Nancy, who were thought to be buried in the cemetery. No specific dates were mentioned, however. The plaque carried the title, *Swing Low, Sweet Chariot.* Needless to say, I jumped in the car and drove right over to see it.

I also continued to study other records at the county library. While searching deeds on microfilm relating to all members of Miles Lassiter's family, I found the record of a final decree in the case of *Anderson Smitherman, et al.,*(especially his wife, Ellen, my great great grandmother) *v. Solomon Kearns, et Ux.* (Ellen's sister Adelaide and her husband) which had been brought before

---

[5] "The Willie Lassiter Petition," *The Genealogical Journal* by the Randolph County Genealogical Society, V, 1 (Winter 1981):38-42.

The People on the Land 59

Figure 5.2: Nancy Dunson grave marker

the Superior Court.[6] After looking at this record, I realized that this was almost certainly referring to the division of lands noted on Ellen's deeds! Now I needed to see the court order itself.

The Final Decree

Back home in Maryland, I looked at the microfilmed records of Superior Court's Orders and Decrees at the Family History

---

[6] *Anderson Smitherman et al, v. Solomon Kearns et Ux*, Deed book 248:156. FHLM #0470851.

Center, and located the court order dated 10 May 1893.[7] None of these documents mentioned the nature of the dispute. Still, it is possible that the dispute arose when Ellen purchased property from their brother Harris Dunson and his wife, Phoebe (Farmer). That land seemed to be in the vicinity of Lassiter Mill. This purchase most likely occurred after the death of their mother, Nancy. Another precipitating factor may have been the death of Colier Lassiter, who seems to have been the family patriarch. Both deaths seem to have occurred in the late 1880s or possibly 1890-92, giving their heirs an opportunity to argue over who should have what. In any event, the information contained in the decree would help to clarify a great deal of information, provide several answers to questions regarding family relationships, and pose new questions. Unfortunately, the precise origins of the property were not revealed by this document. I still didn't know where Healy got her land.

The final decree in this suit, between Grandma Ellen and her husband, Anderson Smitherman (my great great grandfather), and her sister Adelaide, and her husband Solomon Kearns, divided *a home tract and mountain tract* between the heirs of Colier Lassiter, the heirs of Nancy Dunsom [sic], Abigail Lassiter and Jane Lassiter (which seemed to confirm that Colier, Nancy, Abigail and Jane were siblings). The decree did not mention Miles Lassiter or Healy Phillips. Given the size of the overall property and its description as both a mountain tract and home tract, I realized this was almost certainly the same property as that in the estate of Healy Phillips or Lassiter.

I was still confused because Nancy had sold her rights to the property in the June 1851 deed to Colier, therefore technically she shouldn't have received anything. Perhaps the court in 1893 was not provided full background on the ownership of the remaining 365 acres (now known as the Colier Lassiter Tract); or maybe it chose to ignore the fact that Nancy had re-

---

[7] Final Decree, Superior Court Orders and Decrees, 2:308-309. FHLM #0475265.

linquished all claims. The court may have been willing to do this because Nancy and her family members continued to share some of the acreage, living on it and farming it. Thus, since they continued to live as tenants in common, the court awarded them accordingly. Whatever the reason for the court's determination, the fact remains that the court awarded land to my ancestor, Grandma Ellen, as well as her sister, Adelaide, an apparent niece (Mamie Hill) and nephew (Will Dunson), all heirs of Nancy Dunson.

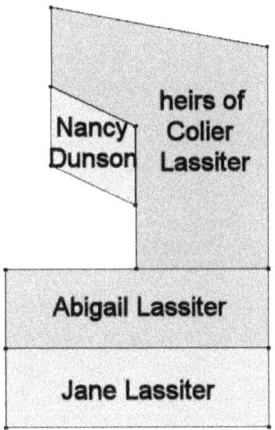

Figure 5.3: Division of Lands of Miles Lassiter

The parcels given in this division to Ellen Smitherman (Grandma Ellen) as a descendant of Nancy Dunson matched precisely those mentioned in the two later deeds of sale to her cousins Will and Colon Lassiter, and called therein part of the *"Division of Lands of Miles Lassiter."*[8] I had found it! None of my cousins was familiar with this decree. They were amazed at this discovery. In fact, because of this document, I now knew about additional family members, identified as descendants of

---
[8] Estate of Miles Lassiter/Charles and Ellen Mayo to Will Lassiter and Colon Lassiter, Deed Book 166:91, FHLM #0470286; and Colon C. Lassiter to Ellen Mayo, Deed Book 163:264, FHLM #0470285.

my great-great-great grandmother, Nancy. It was interesting to realize once again that Kate and her siblings knew so many of the relatives from my direct line, but knew nothing of my mother.

Chapter 6

Family Reunions and Private Papers

Figure 6.1: Lassiter Family Reunion, 1987

The First Reunion

During the summers, on the fourth Sunday in August, and continuing some years for two or three nights, Strieby Church holds homecoming and revival services, as other area churches do on other weekends. These events also serve as family reunions, because many family members from places like New York, Massachusetts, New Jersey, and Florida come home. In 1987, though, the family decided to hold a big reunion on the Fourth of July weekend. It was a huge event, with over 200 people from places as far away as California. We also had members of the family of the (White) Widow Sarah Lassiter. They came anxious to talk about my research and show some pictures of some of the older generations from their side of the family.

The reunion spanned almost the entire weekend. We had a reception for those arriving on Friday. On Saturday we took the kids and others to the North Carolina Zoo and to a pottery-maker in the Seagrove area. Seagrove is renowned for its pottery, with many potters from families whose members have been potters for several generations. Later that day we had a barbecue and picnic, and then later that night, a dance. On Sunday, we had special church services with an address by State Representative, the Honorable H. McKinley Michaux, followed by a luncheon. The Asheboro *Courier-Tribune* sent reporters to cover the event.

For this our first big family reunion, I published my research findings in a small program booklet. Naturally, everyone who came to the family reunion received a copy of the booklet.[1] One of the things I made sure to do was to donate a copy of my publication to several repositories. Since I had copyrighted it, there was a copy at the Library of Congress. I gave a copy to the Family History Library, in Salt Lake City, and to my local Family History Center in Kensington, Maryland, and, of course, I made sure to give a copy to the Randolph County Library. I also forwarded a copy to the Friends Collection at Guilford College.

---

[1] Margo Lee Williams, *The Miles Lassiter Family of Randolph County, North Carolina—A Short Family History* (Silver Spring, Maryland: By the author, 1987).

Letters and Deeds

Over the next few years, Harold Lassiter mentioned from time to time that he had papers which referenced some of these people, including Healy.

He said that the birthdays of Miles' children were recorded therein. He promised to look for them. Finally, one Thanksgiving weekend, he brought the papers from his home in Charlotte. They were kept in a now somewhat deteriorated leather document pouch, and then in a cloth sleeve that is in moderately good condition, though clearly quite old. Included were copies of the original land grant to Christopher Bundy for the 100 acres that Miles first bought from Jesse Morgan then sold to Henry Newby. There was also a copy of a deed that was apparently unrecorded for 9 acres that Colier purchased from William Lassiter.[2] This land was said to adjoin Healy's land. It was amazing to see and hold these old, fragile papers. These papers which had been passed down from the very people I was researching. I was particularly moved by a paper which had been a bill for medical services rendered to my great-great-great grandmother, Nancy. The bill was to Miles and was for $10.00.[3]

Perhaps one of the most interesting pieces was a paper that named seven children and gave their birth dates: Emsley, Susannah, Abigail, Colier, Wiley, Nancy, and Jane. It was like holding something sacred. It was like shaking hands with my ancestors. I was touching the paper that touched the hands...

One of the most significant papers was a letter. In January 1851, Miles' son Colier had apparently consulted J. Worth, a local attorney and Quaker about the family's property. Worth's reply, which was preserved by the family, outlined the facts regarding the family's situation.

> Collier Philips, of color, consults us on the following case—

---
[2] Private papers of Harold Lassiter.
[3] Ibid.

Figure 6.2: Harold Lassiter

He states that he is the son of a free woman of color, named Helia— that she had four children by a first husband and seven by a second husband who was a slave, the said Collier being one of the seven— that his mother died some five years ago possessed of a considerable personal estate, all of which had been acquired after the second marriage— and his father and the children of the second marriage lived together in common till last summer when his father died, no administration having been granted on the estate of his mother: — He further states that one of the seven children lives in the West & wants his

Family Reunions and Private Papers   67

share— and the remaining six do not desire a division in severalty among them—

Upon this state of facts he wishes to know whether the four children are entitled to any thing— And if so what is the best course to be pursued.

There is no doubt but the four children are entitled each to one eleventh part of the personal estate. —

If an administration were now granted on the estate, it would be necessary to sell the property and would be attended by many other inconveniences, as the family are not disposed to divide & live separately.

We advise that the seven buy up with the common fund or means, the interests of the four, if it can be done on reasonable terms. If not, then that some one administer and distribute according to law. —

If the shares of the four be bought, the conveyance ought to be to the seven and the payment should be made out of the common estate. —

If the child in the West has an agent here and the four shares are bought up, then the six may buy up, at an agreed price, the interest of the one in the West, leaving the six who are living together tenants in common of the property.

Jan. 22nd 1851
J. Worth
R. H. B. (? — paper torn very difficult to read)

Thus, examination of this one document revealed that:

- Healy (or *Helia* as she was referred to in this document) had been married before Miles, and had 4 children in that marriage—names unknown

- She was indeed free and Miles had been a slave

- She had amassed the property while married to Miles

- She died approximately 1845, and Miles died in the summer of 1850

- One child lived out west, while the other six lived as tenants in common on the property.[4]

These papers that my cousin Harold had kept confirmed that the Nancy, Wiley, Susannah and Emsley, and Colier mentioned in the deed dated 28 June 1851,[5] were brothers and sisters. Since Emsley was represented by an attorney in this deed, he was probably the child living out west. However, this raised new questions. Since these four were among the seven children had by Miles, why were they selling their rights in the land to Colier?

Also preserved in the family papers was a bond note between Colier Philips and Nancy Philips Lassiter, dated 4 July 1851, wherein he promised to pay her $79.28½ the following day.[6] It does not, however, say for what this bond note was being given. Was it somehow related to the land? It was dated only a few days after the 28 June deed.

Another paper in Harold's collection helped answer the question about what happened to Wiley and Jane. It was a letter Wiley had written to Colier.[7] The letter states that he is living in Fayetteville, North Carolina. He explains that his family, particularly his wife Bettey, are very sick. He takes comfort, however, from the fact that their sister Jane is with them and helping to care for the family. The letter is dated 10 August 1858. Wiley mentions that the family would like to return to Randolph County, but health and lack of money

---

[4] Statement of J. Worth, regarding the consultation by Calier Phillips about the division of the estate of Helia Phillips.

[5] Emsley and Susan Lassiter, et al, to Calier Phillips, Deed Book 29:495. FHLM #0470233.

[6] Private papers of Harold Lassiter.

[7] Ibid.

were preventing them from doing so. Thus, this information contradicted information previously received that Wiley had gone north, perhaps to New York.

When I returned to Maryland, I searched the 1860 census for Cumberland County and found Wiley and family located in Fayetteville.[8] It listed Wiley, Elizabeth, Abigail, Parthania (who may have been the *Parthana* on the 1850 census in Miles' household), Martha (a previously unknown family member), Nancy, Julián (elsewhere spelled *Julia Ann*), and John. Jane was not living with them. Continued searching resulted in locating an appropriate *Jane Lassiter*, in 1870, living as a domestic servant in Salisbury, Rowan County, North Carolina,[9] but no appropriate Wiley Lassiter in Cumberland, Randolph, or Rowan Counties. The 1870 census for Randolph County showed Elizabeth and some of the children had returned to Randolph County,[10] but nothing was found for either Elizabeth or Jane in 1880. Jane was named as an heir in the division of the land, but the heirs of Wiley were not named. This was the last time Jane was mentioned in any of the records so far located. Searches for Susannah have been unproductive, and she was not named as an heir in the final decree that divided the land.

So, many questions still remained:

- Where did Emsley live out west, and did he have any family?

- What happened to Susannah?

- Who were the other four children from Healy's first marriage, and who was her first spouse?

- How did Healy acquire her property?

---

[8] 1860 U.S. Census, Free Inhabitants, Cumberland County, North Carolina, Fayetteville, Wiley Lassiter, NAM #M653-894, 497.

[9] 1870 U.S. Census, Rowan County, North Carolina, Salisbury Township, Jane Lassiter, NAM #M593-1158, 580A.

[10] 1870 U.S. Census, Randolph County, North Carolina, Asheboro Township, Elizabeth Lassiter, NAM #M593-1156, 287A.

Figure 6.3: Lassiter Family Reunion, 1996

The Second Reunion

This is where the research stood in 1996, when we had our second, somewhat smaller, family reunion, for which I published a new reunion booklet with updated information about the family in it.[11] This time I was able to locate some of the descendants of Wiley Lassiter, and acquire some pictures of various branches of the family for inclusion in the updated booklet. In addition, I included pictures from the first reunion. It was during that editorial process that I was struck by how many of those older individuals were no longer living. Again, I donated copies of my reunion booklet to the various repositories, adding this time the libraries of the National Genealogical Society, and the African-American Historical and Genealogical Society (I had previously published an article about the land in the "AAHGS" journal of which I had been an editor),[12] and later, the International Society of the Sons and Daughters of Slave Ancestry.

---

[11] Williams, Second Edition, 1996.
[12] "Division of Lands of Miles Lassiter," *Journal of the Afro-American Historical and Genealogical Society*, Volume 14: 1&2 (1995).

Chapter 7
Still Looking

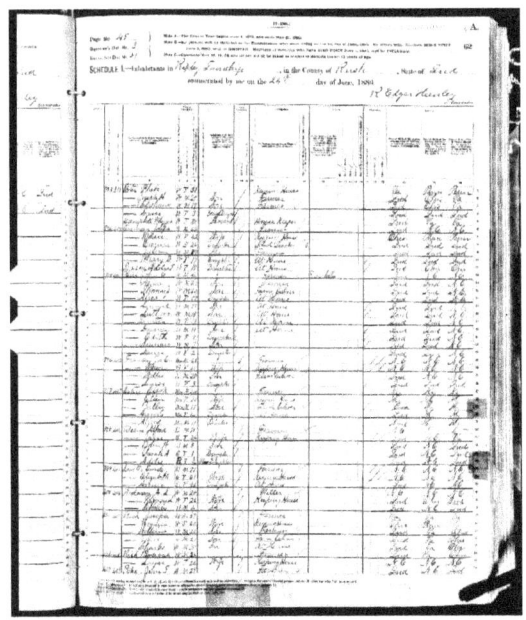

Figure 7.1: Emsley Lassiter 1880 census Indiana, from ancestry.com

Emsley Lassiter

I continued to try to locate information regarding the other questions, including finding out what happened to Emsley, and where out west he might have gone. Answering the question of where Emsley was living "out west," was difficult. Some thought he might have gone as far west as Missouri or Kansas, but searches for leads in those states proved to be dead ends. However, with the publication of the 1880 index and census on CD Rom, by the Family History Library in Salt Lake City, I was able to locate him in the 1880 census living in Ripley, Rush County, Indiana.[1] A search of county records showed that he married Elizabeth Winburn, also from North Carolina (but not Randolph County), in 1845,[2] and that he purchased and sold land belonging to J. T. Thornburg, of Randolph County, North Carolina.[3] I also found in the county records property belonging to a Jesse and Ezekiel Lassiter, also of Randolph County, North Carolina, most likely the grandsons of Sarah, and sons of Micajah.[4] Surely, this was our Emsley. The census noted that Emsley and Elizabeth had a daughter named Ann. What became of Ann I have not been able to learn to date. No marriage record in Rush County has been located, and she does not appear as "Ann Lassiter" in the 1900 census. I also searched probate records for some indication about when Emsley or Elizabeth died, but to no avail.

---

[1] Family Search, 1880 United States Census and National Index, Family History Resource File (Salt Lake City: Church of Jesus Christ of Latter-Day Saints, 2001), Rush County, Indiana, Emsley Lasiter.

[2] Marriage Record of Emsley Lasiter and Elizabeth Winburn, Rush County, Indiana, 1845, FHLM 1630189.

[3] Deed, J. T. Thornburg to Emsley Lassiter, Rush County, Indiana, FHLM #1630184 items 2-3; FHLM #1630186 items 2-3.

[4] Deeds of Jesse and Ezekiel Lassiter, Rush County, Indiana, FHLM #1630184 items 2-3; FHLM #1630186 items 2-3

The Other Children

While answers to questions about Wiley, Emsley, Jane and Susannah have been difficult to find, trying to determine Healy's first husband and her other four children have been even more perplexing, and the potential answers are far from conclusive. A strong candidate for husband is Nathan Phillips, a free man of color found on the 1840 census, in Randolph County, and of appropriate age.[5] In the 1850 census, his probable wife was named as "Hester."[6] Potential children in the household were too young to have been Healy's. However, there were several children identified from apprenticeship and marriage records (also published by *The Genealogical Journal* in 1998), who are potential candidates to be Healy's other four children.

The apprenticeship bonds for the county showed that four children of color were apprenticed on 6 May 1822 and 8 May 1822. On the 6th, Daniel and Charley Phillips were apprenticed to Phineas Nixon, with instructions to not remove these children from the county. On the 8th, Noah and Nathan Phillips (Jr.) were apprenticed to Thomas Nixon and Herman Allen, respectively. Noah was to be taught blacksmithing. Again they were admonished to not remove the children from the county. Apparently Noah Phillips was not brought right away to Nixon's, because in August the sheriff was sent to retrieve him from Hiram Lamb.[7] Nathan Phillips (Jr.) can be eliminated, however, because in a later record his father, Nathan Phillips (Sr.) bound him to Andrew Hoover. Additionally, in another apprenticeship proceeding, Nathan Phillips, the elder, is named as the father of

---

[5] 1840 US Census, South Division, Randolph, North Carolina; NARA M704-369; Page: 65 Family History Library Film: 0018097. Nathan Phillips, of color, head. Retrieved from *Ancestry.com*

[6] 1850 US Census, Southern Division, Randolph, North Carolina; Roll: M432_641; Page: 139A, Nathan Philips, head. Retrieved from *Ancestry.com*.

[7] Carol Lawrence Vidales. (1998) "Randolph County Apprentice Bonds," *The Genealogical Journal* by the Randolph County Genealogical Society, vol XXII (2):56-57.

Nathan Phillips, the boy. In that record Sally Phillips is named as a daughter of Nathan's, again too young to be Healy's[8].

Two other candidates for Healy's children were Micajah Phillips and Susannah Phillips. Micajah Phillips married a woman named Tamer, in 1826.[9] Micajah is mentioned two more times in county records in the 1840s,[10] and is presumed to have died before 1850 when Tamer appears without him, but with several children.[11]

Susannah is mentioned in May 1814. The apprenticeship bonds mention bringing her children to court, calling them her orphans.[12] One child is a girl, Nancy, and the other a boy named Grief. So far, no real evidence to confirm their relationships with Healy has been located, although the coincidence of the names "Susannah," and "Nancy," with the names of Healy's children suggests some possible relationship. However, given that Susannah was already dead in 1814, and Micajah was dead by 1850, they were probably not among the four referenced by J. Worth in his letter above. That leaves Noah, Daniel, and Charley, as possibilities. Who was the fourth? So far, I have found nothing concrete.

---

[8] Carol L. Vidales (1999). "Randolph County, North Carolina Apprentice Bonds, 1842-1844," Volume XXIII(3):7-8, "Two boys of old Nathan Philip's daughter (Sallie) to be bound out at November court...Lorenzo D. Philip, orphan...Franklin Philip, orphan."

[9] Marriage of Micager Phillips and Tamer, 5 Dec 1826. County Court Records at Asheboro, NC and FHL # 0019641, 0019658 and 0418149

[10] Presentment of a grand jury, 11 Sep 1842, against Kid Phillips and Tamer Phillips his wife, "Gleanings from Randolph County Criminal Actions, 1842," (2009). Vol XXXIII(3):45; and 1843, volume XXXIV(3):43. The last known appearance of his name in any county records was the presentment and appearance in the county courts on 26 Jan 1843.

[11] 1850 US Census, Southern Division, Randolph, North Carolina; Roll: M432_641; Page: 139A, Tamer Phillips. Retrieved from *Ancestry.com*.

[12] Carol Lawrence Vidales. (1998) "Randolph County Apprentice Bonds," *Genealogical Journal*, vol XXII(2):54.

Chapter 8

Back to the Land

Figure 8.1: The old barn, Lassiter family farm, Lassiter Mill Road

Due to Bonds

One question still persisted: Where did Healy get the land? I was busy with my job, my daughter's school, and all the myriad things of life, so I wasn't doing a lot of active research. I was still talking to relatives and other researchers, reading various journals for tips, and reading the Randolph County journal to see if I could come up with new strategies for identifying how Healy had acquired the land. Then, in November 2002, I received a letter from Marian Miller of Asheboro. In her letter she noted that she was contacting me because she had seen my publications at the Randolph County Library. She went on to say that she had found information about my family in a deed pertaining to her family and knew I would be interested, and so she was forwarding a copy of the deed to me.

It was a copy of the deed of trust between her ancestor, John Newsom, and Ezekiel Lassiter, Sarah's grandson, with whom the Newsoms lived. It was dated 1840, and recorded in Deed Book 22.[1] It stated that John Newsom owed "Helley Phillips and her heirs or children had by Miles Lassiter... due to bonds for $250." *Due to bonds?* That meant that Healy and her children had posted a bond for Newsom in the amount of $250 (for what purpose it didn't say), and he was now agreeing to pay that money back, which he claimed he would do, and outlined a payment schedule in the deed. To secure that money he put up 150 acres of land along Hannah's Creek, a tributary of the Uwharrie River. Ezekiel Lassiter would be the trustee.

This situation was puzzling. John Newsom was White. Why would he be borrowing money from Healy, a woman of color? It was also interesting to note that he said he owed Healy "and her heirs or children had by Miles Lassiter." He didn't say "her heirs," but rather her "heirs or children had by Miles Lassiter." This could lead one to conclude that it was Miles' money, but, since he was technically Healy's slave, he did not have the legal standing to be "owed" money. Therefore, the deed was worded such that Newsom owed the money to Healy and her "heirs or children had by Miles Lassiter," thus protecting Miles' interests and that of his children, as opposed to her children from her

---

[1] John Newsome to Ezekiel Lassiter, Randolph County Deed Book 22. Proved in court August term 1840, Court of Common Pleas and Quarter Sessions.

previous marriage.

I have found no other deed between Newsom and the Phillips/Lassiters. I have assumed, therefore, that since this land appeared to be referenced in a later deed between Miles' and Healy's son, Wiley Phillips Lassiter and Robert G. Murdock, that Newsom in some way forfeited on the trust, and the land was given by Ezekiel to Healy. In fact, the reference in the court petition of Wiley Lassiter's may not have referred to the time when Healy died (although it may have been about the same time chronologically), but rather to the possible forfeiture and subsequent transfer of property. This is the only transfer of land that I have identified between the White Lassiter family and the Miles Lassiter family. This may be the so-called gift to which descendants of Sarah Lassiter were referring, not knowing that it was only 150 acres, and was not a gift, but apparently repayment for a loan.

In any event, this now meant I could account for 259 acres of the 400 acres mentioned in the 1851 deed between Colier, Nancy, Wiley, Jane, and Emsley, or even the 300 acres referenced in the 1855 deed of trust with Samuel Hill. There was the 100 acres that Miles originally bought from Jesse Morgan, in 1815, sold to Henry Newby, and at some point returned. Then there was the nine acres Colier bought from William Lassiter, adjoining Healy's land, and this land for 150 acres. I asked Harold (who was especially pleased to learn this new information) and Kate about the Newsom's, but while they knew who the family was, they had no knowledge of any particularly close relationship between the families. Nevertheless, it was really gratifying to learn that sending a copy of my work to the historical society had given me back such a huge pay-off.

Land Values and Money

Having looked at these deeds and noted the various sale prices and appraisals of Healy's and Miles' property, I wondered how the value of this estate would translate into today's money. With inflation, what would the cost of this estate be in today's money? The original 100 acres was purchased for $50, in 1815. That would have been equal to $439.27, in 2005. When the 400 acre estate was probated about 1854, it was valued at $802.19. In 2005, that would have been equal to $17791.20. However, the tax rate in 2005 far exceeds that amount, and the appraised value for that acreage is different still.

Putting It Together

I had started out looking for the origins of 11 acres belonging to my great great grandmother, Ellen, and eventually learned that there was close to 400 acres. I was thinking of the land as one parcel, but it had turned out that it was a number of parcels put together. I had identified about 259 acres so far. There was still 100 acres unaccounted for. The only other purchase of land I knew of was the acquisition of 100 acres in a land grant obtained by Wiley Phillips (Lassiter) in 1850. This land was located along Walker's Creek, another Uwharrie tributary. However, this was somewhat curious, since this land should not have been included in any inheritance from Healy.

In any event, at last I had documents which confirmed the marital relationship between Miles and Healy, as well as corroboration of the relationships between each of the children. Despite all my success in identifying these individuals and learning about the land, I would have loved to learn more details about their lives. I had been through so many of the records of the county, repeatedly interviewed relatives and others about the family and the land. I had searched numerous indexes for names relating to this family, and searched numerous genealogical internet websites, databases, and message boards. I had contacted White and Black Lassiters. I had been pretty thorough, or so I thought, and I felt any additional information was probably going to have to fall in my lap unexpectedly. I didn't think I would be able to go much further using standard research techniques. Generally speaking, I felt pretty satisfied. After all, I finally had a pretty good idea where the land came from.

Chapter 9

You Never Know

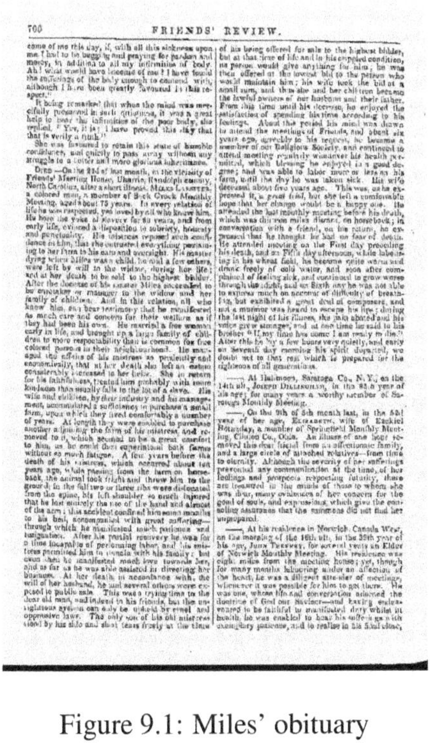

700 FRIENDS' REVIEW.

come of me this day, if, with all this sickness upon me, I had to be begging and praying for pardon and mercy, in addition to all my infirmities of body. Ah! what would have become of me? I have found the sufferings of the body enough to contend with, although I have been greatly favoured in this respect."

It being remarked that when the mind was mercifully preserved in such quietness, it was a great help to bear the infirmities of the poor body, she replied, "Yes, it is; I have proved this day that that is verily a truth."

She was favoured to retain this state of humble confidence, and quietly to pass away without any struggle to a better and more glorious inheritance.

DIED.—On the 23d of last month, in the vicinity of Friends' Meeting House, Uharrie, Randolph county, North Carolina, after a short illness, MILES LASSITER, a colored man, a member of Back Creek Monthly Meeting, aged about 75 years. In every relation of life he was respected, yea loved by all who knew him. He bore the yoke of slavery for 60 years, and from early life, evinced a disposition to sobriety, honesty and punctuality. His mistress reposed such confidence in him, that she entrusted everything pertaining to her farm to his care and oversight. His master dying when Miles was a child, he and a few others, were left by will to the widow, during her life; and at her death to be sold to the highest bidder. After the decease of his master Miles succeeded to be caretaker or manager to the widow and her family of children. And in this relation, all who knew him, can bear testimony that he manifested as much care and concern for their welfare as if they had been his own. He married a free woman early in life, and brought up a large family of children to more respectability than is common for free colored persons in their neighbourhood. He managed the affairs of his mistress so prudently and economically, that at her death she left an estate considerably increased to her heirs. She in return for his faithfulness, treated him probably with more kindness than usually falls to the lot of a slave. His wife and children, by *their* industry and *his* management, accumulated a sufficiency to purchase a small farm, upon which they lived comfortably a number of years. At length they were enabled to purchase another adjoining the farm of his mistress, and removed to it, which seemed to be a great comfort to him, as he could then superintend both farms without so much fatigue. A few years before the death of his mistress, which occurred about ten years ago, while passing from the farm on horseback, the animal took fright and threw him to the ground; in the fall two or three ribs were dislocated from the spine, his left shoulder so much injured that he lost entirely the use of the hand and almost of the arm; this accident confined him some months to his bed, accompanied with great suffering—through which he manifested much patience and resignation. After his partial recovery he was for a time incapable of performing labor, and his mistress permitted him to remain with his family; but even then he manifested much love towards her, and as far as he was able assisted in directing her business. At her death in accordance with the will of her husband, he and several others were exposed to public sale. This was a trying time to the dear old man, and indeed to his friends, but the unrighteous system can only be upheld by cruel and oppressive laws. The only son of his old mistress stood by his side and shed tears freely at the time of his being offered for sale to the highest bidder, but at that time of life and in his crippled condition, no person would give anything for him; he was then offered at the lowest bid to the person who would maintain him; his wife took the bid at a small sum, and thus she and her children became the lawful owners of her husband and their father. From this time until his decease, he enjoyed the satisfaction of spending his time according to his feelings. About this period his mind was drawn to attend the meetings of Friends, and about six years ago, agreeably to his request, he became a member of our Religious Society, and continued to attend meeting regularly whenever his health permitted, which blessing he enjoyed in a good degree; and was able to labor more or less on his farm, until the day he was taken sick. His wife deceased about five years ago. This was, as he expressed it, a *great trial*, but she left a comfortable hope that her change would be a happy one. He attended the last monthly meeting before his death, which was thirteen miles distant, on horseback; in conversation with a friend, on his return, he expressed that he thought he had no fear of death. He attended meeting on the First day preceding his death, and on Fifth day afternoon, while labouring in his wheat field, he became quite warm and drank freely of cold water, and soon after complained of feeling sick, and continued to grow worse through the night, and on Sixth day he was not able to express much on account of difficulty of breathing, but exhibited a great deal of composure, and not a murmur was heard to escape his lips; during the last night of his illness, the pain abated and his voice grew stronger, and at one time he said to his brother "If my time has come I am ready to die." After this he lay a few hours very quietly, and early on Seventh day morning his spirit departed, we doubt not to that rest which is prepared for the righteous of all generations.

——, At Halfmoon, Saratoga Co., N. Y., on the 14th ult., JOSEPH [illegible], in the 85th year of his age; for many years a worthy member of Saratoga Monthly Meeting.

——, On the 9th of 5th month last, in the 53d year of her age, ELIZABETH, wife of Ezekiel [illegible], a member of Springfield Monthly Meeting, Clinton Co., Ohio. An illness of one hour removed this dear friend from an affectionate family, and a large circle of attached relatives—from time to eternity. Although the severity of her sufferings prevented any communication at the time, of her feelings and prospects respecting futurity, there are treasured in the minds of those to whom she was dear, many evidences of her concern for the good of souls, and expressions, which give the consoling assurance that the summons did not find her unprepared.

——, At his residence in Norwich, Canada West, on the morning of the 16th ult., in the 39th year of his age, JOHN [illegible], for several years an Elder of Norwich Monthly Meeting. His residence was eight miles from the meeting house; yet, though for many months labouring under an affection of the heart, he was a diligent attender of meetings, whenever it was possible for him to get there. He was one, whose life and conversation adorned the doctrine of God our Saviour—and having endeavoured to be faithful to manifested duty whilst in health, he was enabled to bear his sufferings with exemplary patience, and to realise in his final close,

Figure 9.1: Miles' obituary

An Obituary

Then something unexpected happened. It was truly serendipity. A friend suggested I should put my own name into an internet search engine. She said I might be surprised to find out what was being circulated as publicly available information. Late one night a few weeks later, early in 2003, I was sitting at the computer and decided to try her suggestion and typed my name into the search window. What came back was somewhat predictable. Since I had been editor of the *Journal of the Afro-American Historical and Genealogical Society*, my name came up in reference to several articles that had been posted on the internet, including the one I had written about Miles and the land. Flattering perhaps, but not shocking or even useful, but now I had another idea. I would search on Miles' name. I really didn't expect anything more than I had gotten dozens of other times. Indeed, at first there were the predictable responses, including my article again. Then suddenly there was something I had never seen before.

There before my eyes was the title of an article about African-American Quakers, by Henry Cadbury, in the *Journal of Negro History*, and an abstract saying that Miles Lassiter was included.[1] I proceeded to the appropriate entry. There I learned the exact date of Miles' death (22 June 1850), and a few details about his life, which it said, had been reported to the person who had written his obituary in *Friends Review*, in 1850! I was shocked, because this article by Cadbury had been written in 1936, and no one, not even the folks at the Friends Historical Society had referred me to it. In fact, it seemed they probably knew nothing about it. Even the book published about Back Creek Friends Meeting, where Miles was a member, made no mention of Miles. No genealogical website that I had searched had returned a reference to this article. Now suddenly, I had

---

[1] Henry Cadbury, "Negro Membership in the Society of Friends" (Part 1), *Journal of Negro History*, 21, 151-213. (1936). <http://www.qhpress.org/quakerpages/qwhp/qwhp.htm>.

his date of death and the information that there was an obituary published at the time of his death.

I was unable to go to the Library of Congress right away. But because I couldn't wait to read the obituary, I contacted a friend who worked there and asked him if he could get a copy and fax it to me.[2] He did. I was stunned. It said that Miles had been "left to the wife of his master" when he was a small child. It went on to talk about his life, his family (although no names were mentioned) and his membership in Back Creek Meeting. I wondered how it had come to pass that over the years Miles had been forgotten—forgotten by history, forgotten by the Quakers, forgotten by his own Meeting. Part of the answer, I believe, lies in the fact that few White researchers really think to look in and among the scholarly works written by people of color. I wondered then, and still wonder: How many other African Americans and other people of color have been similarly forgotten? I didn't know, but I knew I had an opportunity to bring this story to light.

The information in the obituary gave a new framework for analyzing some of the information I had gathered, including Miles' relationship to the White Lassiter family, and his place in North Carolina Quaker history.

Sarah Lassiter's Family Revisited

All official family histories say Sarah (and Josiah) Lassiter had only one son, Micajah. However, in 1783, Sarah was brought before a Grand Jury on charges of bearing two base-born children. She did not name the father.[3] I have not located any records which identify what became of these two children. On the 1779 and 1785 tax lists and on the 1790 census, Sarah appears as head of household, indicating that she was a single fe-

---

[2] Obituary of Miles Lassiter (1850), *Friends' Review*, Volume III:700.

[3] Francine H. Swaim, "Grand Jury Presentments," Op Cit., Volume XVII, Number 2 (1993), 29.

male, in this case, a widow. Her household included one free White male over 16, 6 free White females, and 5 slaves.[4] Who were these people? I have found nothing to identify them, and they are not reflected in any other records which survive that I have found. This may indicate that they were simply White servants living on the property. In the same census, Micajah, her son, is listed as head of his own household. He would have been about 25-30 years of age. His household had two free White males over 16, two free White males under 16, one free White female, and one slave.[5]

As previously mentioned, some descendants of Sarah's son, Micajah, have written that her husband Josiah died in 1778, while others have said he died as late as 1790. The 1790 date is highly improbable, if not impossible, based on the information in the 1779 and 1785 tax lists, and the 1790 census itself, indicating that Sarah was already a widow.

Sarah's probate record seemed to provide no discernible clues to Josiah's existence either. Since she died intestate (without a will), her inventory and estate sale mention nothing about a past husband. The only interesting feature of her estate was that it was probated at the same time as one for an Ezekiel Lassiter, whose entire estate showed only three slaves: Miles, Jack, and Samuel. I thought for a while that Ezekiel had to be one of her grandchildren, even though another Ezekiel, son of Micajah had survived to adulthood.[6] Perhaps it was a child hitherto not accounted for in the known list of Micajah's children. It was not unheard of for people to give more than one child the same first name, and perhaps a different middle name. If this was not the case, then I did not know who this Ezekiel could be. In any event, I have never found any early records in Rowan, Guilford, or Randolph Counties that mention Josiah

---

[4] 1790 U.S. Census, Randolph County, Hillsborough District, Sarah Lassiter, head, 100. NAM #T498-2, item 2.

[5] Ibid., Micajah Lassiter, head.

[6] Ezekiel Lassiter, 21-Dec-1794 - 11-May-1865, Burial: Oak Grove Methodist Church Cemetery, Randolph County, North Carolina.

Lassiter.

Records of Lassiters in Gates County, in eastern North Carolina, are difficult to reconcile with those in Randolph County, except that Sarah's son, Micajah, married his first wife, Celia Spivey, in Gates County.[7] By 1790, however, Micajah and family were living in Randolph County. There was a Josiah Lassiter in Gates County records who died in 1790, however, there is nothing to link him with Sarah and Micajah. While the 1778 death date is more plausible, the presence or identity of any Josiah Lassiter is still elusive. Although this information appears on two websites published by descendants, no information has been presented on those sites to support this scenario.[8]

These two websites claim that Josiah had several siblings. There was not much information provided, except that they were the children of Aaron and Christian (Booth) Lassiter. One site lists their names as: Aaron, Ezekiah (Ezekiel?), Christina, Josiah, Christian, Rose, and Mary. The other website lists all but Christian. This is probably based on a will by Aaron Lassiter in Gates County. That will was written in October 1779,[9] and probated in 1781. In it, Aaron leaves property or gives money to his children, including Josiah. However, if the Josiah of Randolph County died in September 1778, this Aaron of Gates County was probably not his father. It is unlikely that a full year before writing his will that Aaron would not have had word about his son Josiah's death and thus substituted Micajah's name as heir in lieu of Josiah.

---

[7] North Carolina. Division of Archives and History, *An Index to Marriage Bonds Filed in The North Carolina State Archives* (Raleigh: North Carolina Dept Cultural Resources, [1977]?).

[8] Retrieved from: http:// familytreemaker .genealogy .com/ users/h/i/g/ Karen Hight/ WEBSITE0001/ UHP0451 .html?Welcome=1077560931 and Retrieved from: http:// www .brianjacobs .org/ genealogy/ laster/ html/ d0042/ g0000070.html.

[9] Will of Aaron Lassiter, October 1779, Gates County, NC, Will Book 1, p. 11. FHLM #18965.

Miles as Slave Revisited

I learned when I read Miles' obituary, which appeared in *Friends Review*, in 1850, that Miles personally reported that he was given to his master's widow on the condition that when she died, he (Miles) was to be sold.[10] Thus, I learned from his obituary that he was always a slave and never was freed during Sarah's lifetime, despite both what appeared to be contrary evidence in the records I had found, and the family tradition in the families of her descendants.

The obituary went on to say that he had become the manager and overseer for the Widow Lassiter and her family. According to the account therein, he had been very successful in this position and had significantly improved her family's financial well-being. It mentioned also that he was injured in a riding accident. The accident left him permanently disabled, nevertheless, the Widow continued to rely on him to manage her affairs. The obituary also stated that Miles and his wife, a free woman of color, acquired land adjacent to the Widow's land, and that he then managed both properties.

How curious, even amazing, Miles was born a slave, yet rose to such a level of competence and confidence that he would be the manager/overseer of his owner's property. He would even enjoy some of the perquisites of the status of a free man by purchasing his own property and being listed as a free man in the 1830 census. Miles may have even learned some minimal reading and math skills to help him in his managerial duties. In other words, Miles (and probably his brothers) may have been treated *as if* he (and they) were free, even if he was not free. Thus, it seems he enjoyed freedom and opportunity without having to leave his community or his owner's oversight. What circumstance might possibly lend itself to such a scenario?

---

[10] Obituary of Miles Lassiter (1850), Friends' Review, Volume III:700.

Blood Relations

The Lassiter Mill area of Randolph County continues to be primarily a rural, farming and lumbering community. Until very recently, despite other forms of segregated living (church or school) descendants of both Sarah's family and Miles' family have labored side by side, helping each other on their farms, helping each other with planting and harvesting, even supporting each other in times of important life events, such as birth or death. Over the years, some of Sarah Lassiter's descendants have told Miles' family members that the two families are blood relatives. In support of that premise, I noted again that Sarah was charged with bastardy in 1783 for the birth of two children. Since those children cannot be accounted for among her White descendants, I wondered if one of them could be Miles. Although the 1783 date seems to support more closely that Jack and Samuel were possibly her children, I still wondered if Miles, Jack *and* Samuel were her children.

Her children? That might explain it. Other White parents of the mixed-blood children of their slaves have given those children opportunities not usually available to the average slave. If Miles, Jack and Samuel were the children of Sarah Lassiter, then Miles' opportunities and privileges would be plausible. If it were true that she had three children then that would indicate that she was not just indiscrete, but rather that she was in fact in a long term relationship with an African-American male, possibly even one of her slaves.

How or why? The farm and mill were located in the country, about 12-15 miles from the town (now city) of Asheboro, the current county seat (and even farther from the previous county seat of Johnsonville). In the 1770s this was a significant distance. For a widow, this rural, somewhat isolated, sometimes lonely, lifestyle had (has) the potential for allowing, even supporting, unconventional relationships. Relationships that would not have withstood the scrutiny of life in town, had space and privacy in the country. In addition, a widow who was possessed of some considerable wealth would not suffer the opprobrium that might face others with less wealth and presumed influence who engaged in such an unconventional and unacceptable relationship. This illicit relationship may have prospered, especially while Sarah's legitimate son, Micajah, had gone east in search of his own bride.

In any event, by the time Sarah died her probate record showed that she did not own any slaves. This would have been consistent with the statement in Miles' obituary that Sarah was to have possession of Miles as long as she lived and then, in accordance with her husband's will, he would have to be sold. However, repeated searches did not identify a Lassiter will from this time period. Because the estate of an Ezekiel Lassiter was being probated at the same time as Sarah's (with Miles, Jack, and Samuel listed as his property), I even speculated that Sarah's own estate may not have been probated at the time of her death but later, in 1840, at the time of the death of a possible grandson Ezekiel Lassiter (perhaps even the one to whom she had sold her property),[11] or so I thought. Only after re-evaluating this probate record in light of Miles' obituary, did I realize that the Ezekiel whose estate was being probated at the same time as Sarah's was perhaps a different, and as yet inadequately identified Ezekiel.

Now I wondered: What if Miles' owner's name was Ezekiel, and not Josiah? That would mean that Sarah was Ezekiel's wife, not Josiah's, and Micajah was Ezekiel's son, not Josiah's; or possibly his name was Josiah Ezekiel, or Ezekiel Josiah. Remember what I said about not jumping to conclusions. I based that on the information from Miles' obituary which said that upon the death of his master, he was to be given to his master's

---

[11] Letters of Administration: Sarah Lassiter and Ezekiel Lassiter, and Order to sell slaves, February 1840, Minutes of the Court of Common Pleas and Quarter Sessions FHLM #0019652 or #0470211. See also Will Book 7: (Sarah and Ezekiel) Inventory, 303; (Sarah) Account, 331; (Ezekiel) Account, 332; (Sarah and Ezekiel) Final Distribution of the Estate, 406. FHLM #0019643.

widow.

Assuming this Ezekiel was Sarah's husband, based on the obituary, he was still alive when Miles was born. Would he have been so invalided that he did not know of his wife's indiscretions? Was he aware but somehow powerless or otherwise unwilling to do anything? Was Miles perhaps Ezekiel's child, or Micajah's child? I believe it is unlikely that he was Ezekiel's child because wives, and even more so widows, are not willing to treat the children of their husband's indiscretions with exceptional favors. Was he Micajah's child (born before he married Celia Spivey), and therefore Ezekiel and Sarah's *grandchild*? A slave grandchild can be moved into the home of the White slave-owning grandparents who bestow special treatment and opportunity. What about Jack and Samuel? That is much more difficult to analyze. Far less information is available concerning these two men. They were born about the time Sarah was accused of giving birth out of wedlock. On the other hand, both men were born before Micajah married Celia Spivey. Perhaps all three were her grandchildren. In any event, both men, like Miles, were given privileges. Finally, both men, along with Miles, were handled in the same way by Ezekiel's estate.[12]

Was Ezekiel actually the elusive Josiah, Sarah's husband? Miles' obituary went on to say that upon her death, he, Miles, should be sold. I realized that Miles (and his brothers) were the only property listed in Ezekiel's estate. It seemed plausible that this meant that Miles and his brothers were being returned to the estate of their owner for sale, since they had never been owned by Sarah, only a trust during her lifetime. What about Ezekiel's other property? That property had rightfully passed to Sarah, the widow, and was now being sold from her estate, with the exception of the real property which she had already sold

---

[12] This line of reasoning would later be proved wrong when Y-DNA testing by Family Tree-DNA would show that Miles clearly descended from an African male of the Haplogroup E3a, the most common DNA lineage among African Americans.

to her grandson, Ezekiel. In addition, after re-examining the final accounting of both estates (which were both being administered by Isaac Keearans), there was mentioned, in reference to Ezekiel's estate, that a will had been "annexed." Apparently the will no longer survives in county records. This re-evaluation of the evidence has led me to believe that Sarah's husband was this Ezekiel Lassiter, who may or may not have had the additional name of *Josiah*. I believe this will greatly affect future research efforts to identify the families of origin of Sarah and her husband.

Sold Into Freedom

As noted before, Ezekiel's probate record showed that he owned three male slaves: Miles, Samuel, and Jack. Miles was bought by "Heley Phillips, col'd," for *five cents*, and Jack by "Colier, col'd," for $12.50, but Samuel was sold to Sawney Cranford for $262.25, in order to recoup losses incurred from Samuel's recapture as a runaway in Raleigh.[13] As mentioned previously, Heley was Miles' wife, a free woman of color. Colier was their son. Again, according to the obituary, Miles had stated that on the day of the sale, Sarah's son Micajah stood with him crying while Miles was offered for sale.

Was he crying at seeing his brother or son offered for sale as Ezekiel (Josiah?) had requested? Why cry? He could have easily afforded to buy him from the estate. The obituary stated that no one would bid for Miles. Was that because people knew that Micajah really didn't want to sell him? Perhaps Micajah really wanted to give Miles his freedom. Under other circumstances he could have freed him and his brothers, since they were over 50. He could certainly have freed Miles for meritorious service as the law allowed, but he had returned him and his brothers to his father Ezekiel's estate for sale.

---

[13] Estate of Ezekiel Lassiter, Account of Sale, Will Book 7:332, FHLM #0019643.

In years past they might have been able to sell him to the Quakers who would have arranged for his freedom, but that was not legally an option any longer. Micajah's tears may have been symbolic of his fear and anxiety as to what kind of person would purchase Miles and how he would be treated. Thus, he probably believed that the only option left was to allow Miles' wife to purchase him. In fact, he may have been relieved that no one bid for Miles at higher prices and his tears may have been an expression of that. In any event, since Miles was purchased by Healy Phillips, it was now her name that appeared as the free head of household in the 1840 census. Presumably she was the female between the ages of 55-100 and he the male between the ages of 55-100, residing therein.[14]

The Land Revisited

Miles and Healy acquired a significant amount of property together. By the time Healy died, they had 409 acres. When the estate was probated after Miles' death, it was found to be worth over 800 dollars.

I originally believed that Miles' land was one parcel, but it turned out to be several parcels acquired over time. As mentioned above, Miles bought 100 acres of land from Jesse Morgan in 1815. This land originated in a land grant from North Carolina to Christopher Bundy, a Quaker. In 1826 Miles, with Sarah Lassiter as a co-grantor, sold the same 100 acre tract to Henry Newby (also a Quaker).[15] Again, as previously noted, sometime before 1857, the 100-acre tract of land bought from Jesse Morgan and sold to Henry Newby found its way back into the hands of the Lassiter family.

---

[14] 1840 US census, Randolph County, North Carolina, Heley Phillips, p. 65. NAM #M704-369.

[15] Jesse Morgan to Miles Lassiter, Deed Book 13:402 (FHLM #0019634 or #0470228); and Sarah and Miles Lassiter to Henry Newby, Deed Book 17:256.(FHLM #0019636 or #0470229).

Quakers involved with the abolitionist movement are reported to have sometimes bought land on which freed slaves could live in peace. Henry Newby may have done this for Miles, or Colier. Why Sarah Lassiter did not become the custodian of this property is unknown, but Miles' association with Newby was possibly relatively close and may have been one of the influences for Miles to become a Quaker himself. One reason Sarah (who was not a Quaker) may not have become custodian is that she was getting older and had herself given over her property to her grandson, Ezekiel. Recognizing that she was approaching the end of her life and would no longer be able to protect his interests, she may have brokered this sale in an effort to secure the property for Miles and his family. However, there is no tangible information about how the land got back into the family's hands.

Additional parcels of land were acquired by the family after Miles was bought by Healy. One of these parcels was acquired by Healy, according to an 1840 deed, when John Newsom put up 155 acres as collateral against a bond, which Healy and her children by Miles Lassiter had paid for him. Ezekiel (Micajah's son) Lassiter was the trustee for this matter. What happened is not clear, but the land did pass to Healy. These parcels eventually amounted to 400 acres.

Miles' final years as a Quaker

On 25 March 1845, Miles requested to be received into the Back Creek Monthly Meeting. His request was confirmed in June of the same year. He became an active and respected member as indicated by the minutes of Back Creek Meeting. His name was last recorded in the minutes in 1850.[16] Miles died on 22 June 1850. Miles was actually a member of Uwharrie Meeting, which was considered a preparatory meeting, and located physically closer to where he lived. Uwharrie Meeting never became an official "Monthly Meeting," so all memberships are officially recorded as part of Back Creek Meeting. As another preparatory meeting in the Little River area grew in size, Uwharrie lost members and was discontinued in 1864. However, Back Creek Meeting is still operative.

Although the association of Quakers with the manumission of slaves and subsequently with the free Black community was well known and close, African Americans were not generally admitted formally to Meetings in North Carolina prior to the Civil War. Miles' admission was all the more remarkable, according to Carole Treadway, bibliographer of the Friends Historical Collection, at Guilford College, in Greensboro, because the minutes did not indicate that he was an African American (or mixed-race) man. In fact, race was not even mentioned as a topic of consideration for his membership, even though race was a specific and volatile issue in the admission of Isaac Linegar to the Deep River Meeting, located in neighboring Guilford County, according to Ms. Treadway.[17] The possibility that a different, White Miles was being reflected in the Back Creek minutes was ruled out because there is no other Miles Lassiter who has been identified as living in Randolph County in this time period. Henry Cadbury discussed Linegar's struggle in his study of African American Quakers.[18] The differences in the two cases are striking. When Linegar requested membership in

---

[16] Back Creek Monthly Meeting Minutes, Volume II, 1840-1870, transcribed in Letters from Carole Treadway, bibliographer, Friends Historical Collection, Guilford College, Greensboro, NC, to Margo Williams, dated 30 Oct 1987, and 25 Nov 1987. See also Hinshaw's *Encyclopedia of American Quaker Genealogy*, North Carolina, "Miles Lassiter" I:723.

[17] Treadway letter, 30 October 1987.

[18] Henry Cadbury, "Negro Membership in the Society of Friends" (Part 1), *Journal of Negro History*, 21, 151-213. (1936), <http://www.qhpress.org/quakerpages/qwhp/qwhp.htm>.

Deep River Meeting, it took over two years before his membership was finally approved. By contrast, Miles' membership was approved in three months. Linegar's case revolved around race, Miles' racial identity was not even noted.

Again, what kind of man was Miles that he was accepted so easily? Certainly, he appears to have been a man of integrity as well as having good business acumen. Perhaps the Linegar case had truly paved the way, at least in this community. If, on the other hand, he was the son of a well-to-do landowner, that probably had an influence on his ability to develop his potential, to acquire and use skills others might not have had, making his acceptance easier. Regardless, it is apparent that he was well respected. Indeed, Cadbury reports that he was the only African-American Quaker in North Carolina, at the time, yet the absence of any notation regarding his race has meant that his presence at Back Creek has effectively been forgotten. When the history of Back Creek Meeting was recently published, there was no mention of Miles among the biographies of notable members, nor mention of Miles in the section regarding relationships with slaves. Miles' easy acceptance, for whatever reasons, seems to have relegated him to historical oblivion.

Curiously enough, there seems to be no evidence that Healy was a Quaker. Since it was not acceptable to be married to a non-Quaker, her non-membership may have been the reason Miles did not pursue membership until after her death. Perhaps she was reluctant to be a Quaker. There are no records identified thus far which can answer that question, and we may never know. The family reports that Miles' son, Colier, was an active Quaker throughout his life. Although no record has been located to date of Colier's involvement, (perhaps also because his wife was not Quaker) his descendants report he was buried in the old Uwharrie Cemetery, the Quaker cemetery for those in the Uwharrie Meeting community, and they believe Miles was buried there as well. The family did not continue its Quaker relationship, however, but went on to become founding members of Strieby and Salem Congregational Churches, and St. Mark's

Methodist Church, and active members of many other denominations.

Chapter 10

It's Never Finished

Figure 10.1: Vella Lassiter, Margaret Williams, Will Lassiter

Despite my many discoveries, I still have questions, about Miles, about Healy, about their children, about other descendants, and about the land. I am still seeking information, and I hope this book may elicit information from anyone who might know something about any of the people named herein. In fact, just as I was ready to publish this book I was able to confirm information that Nancy's daughter Rebecca was indeed the mother of William and her daughter Martha was indeed married to Julius Hill and mother of Mamie Hill. So I hope this story will inspire others to seek their own lost stories.

There is one piece to this lost story I believe I have figured out. Over the years since that first trip to North Carolina I wondered how it was that my mother, her grandmother, and other aunts and uncles seemed to have severed their ties with Colier's descendants, and other descendants of Nancy's who continued to live in the area. This is a close, loving family that always makes room and seemingly, always overlooks human frailty, for the sake of family bonds. So, what happened? I now speculate that it was the land. The very land that has been the glue for so many family members became the source of separation when one sister (Ellen) sued the other (Adelaide) over ownership and control of the land. My guess is, family members took sides in the dispute, with my immediate relatives slowly becoming alienated. If that was the case, I am sorry that their dispute kept me from knowing this large, loving, strong family during my childhood, but I am grateful to my research for making it possible for me to come home, and to be able to pass this legacy on to my daughter.

Figure 10.2: Margo and Turquoise Williams

Part II
A Genealogical Record

Chapter 11

Some Descendants of Miles Lassiter

During their life together, Miles and Healy had seven children: Emsley, Abigail, Colier, Susannah, Wiley, Nancy, Jane. Somewhat atypically, none of these children came before the courts to be apprenticed, nor have any freedom papers been identified that were issued in their names. Certainly, the large Lassiter farm and mill provided work and training opportunities, making apprenticeship unnecessary, but it is also possible that it was yet another example of the privilege this family seemed to enjoy because of its association with the Widow Sarah Lassiter.

Among the papers in the possession of great grandson, Harold Lassiter, was another undated—but clearly old— document which listed the names and birth dates of all seven children.[1] These dates do not correspond precisely with most of the dates reported in the various census listings. However, since this document appears to be contemporary and was kept with the various deeds and letters of the family, I have given it greater weight than the census reports. Descendants of these children continue to live in the Lassiter Mill area, as well as other parts of Randolph County, North Carolina, and elsewhere

---

[1] Handwritten birth record in papers of the late Harold Lassiter.

in the United States.

Miles Lassiter and Healy Phillips

1. Miles Lassiter was born between 1775-1777 in Lassiter's Mill, New Hope, Randolph, NC, and died 22 June 1850 in Lassiter Mill, New Hope, Randolph, NC.[2] He married Healy Phillips (see person number 2, below), a free woman, about 1810 in New Hope, Randolph, NC.

2. Healy Phillips was born about 1780 in North Carolina,[3] and died about 1845 in Lassiter Mill, New Hope, Randolph, NC.[4] Healy had been married before and had four children from that marriage. Miles and Healy had seven children together.[5]

Miles had been born a slave, the property of Ezekiel and Sarah Lassiter. Miles was an overseer for the Lassiter farm. He was purchased from the estate of Ezekiel Lassiter in 1840, by his wife, Healy.[6] Together Miles and Healy were able to acquire more than 400 acres of land.[7] On 25 June 1845, most likely after the death of Healy, Miles was received into Back Creek Friends Meeting.[8] He died on 22 June 1850, the only known

---

[2] Statement of J. Worth, 21 January 1851, Original Letter is in the papers of the late Harold Lassiter, Charlotte, NC. Henry Cadbury, "Negro Membership in the Society of Friends," *Journal of Negro History*, 21 (1936), 180-209, Retrieved from: http://www.qhpress.org/quakerpages/qwhp/bcjnh3.htm; "Miles Lassiter Obituary," *Friends Review*, iii (1850), 700.

[3] 1840 US Census, Randolph County, (NAM #M704-369), 65, Heley Phillips, head.

[4] Statement of J. Worth, 21 January 1851, Worth states that "Helia" died about five years before.

[5] Statement of J. Worth, 21 January 1851, Worth reports that Collier Phillips who was her son was the son of her second marriage to a slave, and that Collier was one of seven children from that marriage. Randolph County, North Carolina, Record of Deeds Book 22, 1839-1841, FHL #19368, pp. 356-357, John Newsom to Ezekiel Lassiter (Deed of Trust), 20 June 1840, "Helley Phillips & her heirs or children had by Miles Lassiter..."

[6] Estate of Ezekiel Lassiter, Will Book 7:332 (FHLM #0019643).

[7] Statement of J. Worth, 21 January 1851.

[8] Hinshaw's *Encyclopedia of American Quaker Genealogy*, North Carolina, "Miles Lassiter" I:723.

African-American Quaker in North Carolina at that time.[9] He was buried at Uwharrie Friends Cemetery.

The First Generation

Children of Miles Lassiter and Healy Phillips

- Emsley Lassiter (see person number 3, below)
- Abigail Lassiter (see person number 5)
- Colier Lassiter (person number 6)
- Susannah Lassiter (person 9)
- Wiley Lassiter (person 10)
- Nancy Lassiter (person 12)
- Jane Lassiter (person 15)

3. **Emsley Lassiter** was born on 01 May 1811 in New Hope, Randolph, NC. He died after 1880 in Ripley, Rush, Indiana. He married Elizabeth Winburn (see person number 4, below) on 03 April 1845 in Rush County, Indiana.

4. **Elizabeth Winburn** was born in 1819 in North Carolina. She died after 1880 in Ripley, Rush, Indiana.

5. **Abigail Lassiter** was born September 1812 in New Hope, Randolph, NC;[10] died 1920 in New Hope, Randolph, NC.[11] She was buried at Strieby Congregational UCC Church,

---

[9] Miles Lassiter Obituary, *Friends Review*, iii (1850), 700.

[10] Handwritten birth record in papers of late Harold Lassiter.

[11] 1910 US Census, Randolph County, North Carolina (NAM #T624-1198), S.D. 7, E.D. 87, Sheet 1A & B, dwelling/family 11, Winston Lassiter, head, "Abbie–Aunt". Abbie does not appear in the 1920 census. Her death and burial were confirmed by Kate Lassiter Jones, Vella Lassiter and Will Lassiter during talks and a visit with them at their home in Asheboro, North Carolina, in September 1982.

Figure 11.1: Abigail Phillips Lassiter ceramic pot

Strieby, NC.[12] She never married. She is first recorded by name living in Miles' household in 1850.[13] She then lived in her brother Colier's household until his death,[14] and continued living with Colier's widow and his son, Winston, and his family[15] until her death, circa 1920. Other than the census records that track her by name from 1850 to 1910, few other records were found relating to her. She was mentioned in the probate of Healy Phillips as an heir and again in the 1893 decree. She

---

[12] There is no tombstone, however, Kate Lassiter Jones confirms her burial here.

[13] 1850 US Census, free schedule, Randolph County, North Carolina, Miles Lassiter, p. 136. NAM #432-641.

[14] 1860 US Census, Randolph County, North Carolina, Colier Lassiter, p. 148, NAM #M653-190; 1870 US Census, Randolph County, North Carolina, Colier Lassiter, p. 24, NAM #M593-1156; and 1880 US Census, Randolph County, North Carolina, Colier Lassiter p. 1, NAM #T9-978.

[15] 1900 US Census, Randolph County, North Carolina, Winson [sic] Lassiter, New Hope Township, sheet 1, S.D. 7, E.D. 90, dwelling 15, family 16, NAM #T623-1213; and 1910 US Census, Randolph County, North Carolina, Winston Lassiter, New Hope Township, S.D. 7, E.D. 87, sheet 1A, dwelling/family 11: "Abbie–Aunt" Sheet 1B, NAM #T624-1198.

sold her allotment to her nephews, Ulysses Winston Lassiter and Amos Barzilla Lassiter, in 1898.[16] Although descendants report that she died approximately 1920, her death was not reported to the state, and there is no official death certificate. She was not recorded in the 1920 census. She is reportedly buried in the Strieby Congregational Church Cemetery.[17]

6. Colier Lassiter was born on 06 November 1815 in New Hope, Randolph, NC.[18] He died in 1887 in New Hope, Randolph, NC.[19] Colier met Laura Ann Williams (person 7). He married Katherine Polk (person 8) on 26 September 1854 in Asheboro, Randolph, NC.[20]

Colier's name first appeared in county records when he bought the freedom of Jack Lassiter from the estate of Ezekiel Lassiter in 1840.[21] In 1850, his name, along with those of his sisters Abigail, Nancy, and Jane appeared in the census listed in the household of Miles Lassiter.[22] In the 1860, 1870, and 1880 censuses,[23] respectively, his name appeared as the head

---

[16] Abigail Lassiter to Winston Lassiter and Amos Barzilla Lassiter, Deed Book 90:268. FHLM #047255.

[17] Strieby Congregational United Church of Christ Cemetery is in Strieby, Union Township, Randolph County. There is no tombstone for Abigail. Her death and burial were confirmed by Kate Lassiter Jones, Vella Lassiter and Will Lassiter during talks and a visit with them in September 1982.

[18] Handwritten birth record in possession of Harold Lassiter.

[19] Randolph County North Carolina, Deeds, 38:288, 1887. "Abigail, Colier, and Kate Lassiter to Jenny Lassiter." This is the last known record of Colier Lassiter. By 1893 his land was embroiled in a lawsuit and divided and distributed to his heirs in "Anderson Smitherman et al v. Solomon Kearns et Ux." Deed Book 248:156.

[20] Randolph County Marriage Records, Book 1:160. See also Ancestry.com. *North Carolina Marriage Bonds, 1741-1868* [database on-line] 2000, and *North Carolina Marriage Collection, 1741-2004* [database on-line] 2007, *Family History Library microfilm # 0475239*.

[21] Estate of Ezekiel Lassiter, Will Book 7:331. FHLM #0019643.

[22] 1850 US Census, free schedule, Randolph County, North Carolina, Miles Lassiter, p. 136. NAM #432-641 or FHLM #444654, item 2.

[23] 1860 US Census, free schedule, Randolph County, NC, Colier Lassiter, p. 148 (NAM #M653-910); 1870 US Census, populations schedule, Randolph County, North Carolina, Colier Lassiter, p. 24. (NAM #M593-1156);

of his own household. After the death of Miles in 1850, Colier seemed to become the head of the extended family, taking responsibility for the homestead (later known as the "Colier Lassiter Tract" in the land records of the county).

In 1848, an unrecorded deed in the possession of Harold Lassiter indicates that he bought land adjacent to his mother's land from William Lassiter, one of Sarah Lassiter's descendants. The land was described as:

> being...on the Est side of the Uharie River beginning at a rock in the middle of the River then East with Thornburgs line to Healy Phillips corner then South with said Phillipses line to a gum then west to a rock in the middle of the River then up the middle of the River to the beginning, half a acre more or less...

The first recorded deed on the inherited land (recorded in 1855) was the 1851 deed where Nancy, Susannah, Emsley, and Wiley sold him all rights to 400 acres.[24] In 1855 he took his first deed of trust on 300 acres,[25] subsequent to the filing of his mother's probate, with whom the land apparently originated.[26] In 1874, he and his wife, Katherine, sold one acre to the Board of Education.[27] His final transaction took place in 1887 when he took a mortgage with a Jenny Lassiter.[28]

---

and 1880 US Census, population schedule, Randolph County, North Carolina, Colier Lassiter, p. 1 (NAM #T9-978).

[24] Emsley and Susan Lassiter, et al, to Calier Phillips, Deed Book 29:495. FHLM #0470233.

[25] Colier Lassiter to Samuel Hill (Tr), Deed Book 30:15. FHLM #0470234.

[26] Estate of Healy Phillips or Lassiter, Will Book 10:190-192. FHLM #0019645.

[27] Colier and Katie Lassiter to Board of Education, Deed Book 38:288. FHLM #0470237.

[28] Abigail, Colier and Kate Lassiter to Jenny Lassiter, Deed Book 56:430. FHLM #0470244.

By 1893 the land was embroiled in the dispute between his nieces Adelaide Kearns and Ellen Smitherman and their husbands. Colier, himself, was dead by this time. His heirs were allotted 150 acres in the final decree.[29]

Additional land records which have been preserved by Colier's descendants include: an 1808 deed from Elijah Bingham to William Arnold for one hundred acres; a land grant (#2406) to Christopher Bundy in 1801,with another copy of the same grant dated 1818 also for one hundred acres "on the waters of the Uharie;" and finally there is a plat and description for eighteen acres of land, location not mentioned but identified as "Calier Lassiter's Clearing," containing an upper piece of 9 acres and 4 rods, and a lower piece of 9 acres and 59 rods.

Colier's name also appeared in a number of other records. In the minutes for the May 1851 term of the Court of Common Pleas and Quarter Sessions, Colier's name (as "Calyer Phillips") was listed on a charge of "bastardy," but no other details were provided.[30] The file, however, listed "Lorey Ann Williams" as mother, and said that the child was born in November 1850.[31] In the Spring of 1857, he was charged in Superior Court with unlawfully carrying firearms.[32] In 1867 his name (recorded as "Calvin") appeared in the records of the Bureau of Refugees, Freedmen and Abandoned Lands (Freedmen's Bureau) as a delegate to the Constitutional Congress for North Carolina.[33] It was at these Congresses in each of the southern states that dele-

---

[29] Anderson Smitherman et al v. Solomon Kearns, et Ux, Final Decree, Deed Book 248:156. FHLM #0470851.

[30] Calyer Phillips, Bastardy Bond, May Term 1851, Minutes of the Court of Common Pleas and Quarter Sessions. FHLM #0019652 or #0470212.

[31] "Bastardy Bonds, 1850-1859," *The Genealogical Journal* by the Randolph County Genealogical Society, XVIII, 2 (Fall 1994): 16. North Carolina State Archives call number, C.R. 081.102.5.

[32] State v. Colier P. Lassiter, Spring Term 1857, Minutes of the Superior Court. FHLM #0470215.

[33] Delegates to the Constitutional Congress, North Carolina, Lassiter Mills District, "Calvin Lassiter," Bureau of Refugees, Freedmen and Abandoned Lands. NAM #M843 roll 32:107.

gates voted each state back into the Union and pledged to uphold the Constitution of the United States.

Colier died sometime between 1887 and 1893. He was reportedly buried at Uwharrie Friends Cemetery, Asheboro.[34] As was common at the time in this heavily Quaker community, his grave was unmarked.

7. Laura Ann Williams was born on 07 January 1831 in Randolph County, NC.[35]

Figure 11.2: Granny Kate Polk Lassiter

8. Katherine Polk was born on 07 March 1832 in Ran-

---

[34] In testimony from granddaughter, Novella A. Lassiter, September 1982, (erroneously reported as "Union cemetery" in earlier publications of this genealogy). The author has visited the cemetery, however, (located on State Road 1107) where many Quakers from the time period are buried, including Samuel Hill, a trustee in the 1855 deed, whose descendants placed a memorial marker in the cemetery.

[35] Carol L. Vidales, Randolph County, North Carolina Apprentice Bonds, 1840-1841, *The Genealogical Journal* by the Randolph County Genealogical Society, Volume XXIII:2, pp. 7,8, Nov 1840: "Sheriff to bring children of color, Laure Ann Williams, -10, & Martiba Williams, -8; 1 Feb 1841: Commissioner Drake, Master: Wm Burney, bond with Jesse Walker not to remove from county; child: Laura Ann E. Williams, orphan 10, 7th last month."

dolph, NC. She was the daughter of Mary "Polly" Polk. She died on 19 December 1906 in Lassiter Mill, New Hope Township, Randolph County, North Carolina, and is buried in the Strieby Congregational Church Cemetery, in the Strieby area of neighboring Union township.[36] Katherine was a founding member of Strieby Church.

9. Susannah Lassiter was born 03 October 1817 in Randolph County, North Carolina.[37] Very little is known about her except that she sold her interest in the family property to Colier in 1851. However, the Worth document indicates that she was living as tenant in common.

10. Wiley Lassiter was born on 13 May 1820 in New Hope, Randolph, NC.[38] He died after 1860 in Fayetteville, Cumberland, NC.[39] He married Elizabeth Ridge[40] (person 11) in 1845 in Asheboro, Randolph, NC.[41]

Wiley's name only appeared once in the census records of Randolph County, in 1850.[42] He was the head of the household, which included his wife Elizabeth and two small children: Abigail, age 4, and Nancy, age 1. He was enumerated close by his father, Miles Lassiter, and his household, and near his uncle, Jack Lassiter, and his family. Besides the 1850 census, there are only two public records that document Wiley's relationship with this Lassiter family: the probate record of Healy Phillips,[43]

---

[36] Tombstone: "Katie, wife of Calier Lassiter," Strieby Congregational United Church of Christ Cemetery, Strieby Church Road, Strieby, Union Township. Her birth is recorded there as 7 March 1832.

[37] Handwritten birth record in possession of Harold Lassiter.

[38] Handwritten birth record in possession of Harold Lassiter.

[39] Last found living in Fayetteville in 1860 census.

[40] Randolph County, North Carolina Marriage Registers., 3:42, Marriage record of her daughter (Nancy) Jane Lassiter to Thomas Bryant, listed her maiden name as "Betsy Ridge."

[41] Henry Cadbury, "Negro Membership in the Society of Friends," *Journal of Negro History*, 21 (1936), 180-209, Retrieved from the World-wide Web: http://www.qhpress.org/quakerpages/qwhp/bcjnh3.htm.

[42] 1850 US Census, free schedule, Randolph County, North Carolina, Willie Lassiter, p. 136. NAM #432-641, or FHLM #444654, item 2.

[43] Estate of Healy Phillips or Lassiter, Will Book 10:190-192. FHLM

and the 1851 deed, where he and his sisters Nancy and Susannah, and brother Emsley, gave their rights to 400 acres to their brother Colier.[44] He moved sometime around 1858 to Fayetteville, North Carolina, and probably died there.

In 1856, Wiley brought suit in the Superior Court and Court of Equity of Randolph County against Michael Bingham.[45] The petition was a counter suit to Michael Bingham's which had won seven judgments against Wiley for money owed amounting to over $600. Wiley's petition charged that he had put carriages and horses on sale at Bingham's store in exchange for goods but that Bingham never properly reconciled the accounts. The result was that Wiley was continuously in debt to Bingham. Wiley was now asking the courts to resolve the issue.[46]

In the petition Wiley mentioned having acquired two tracts of land: one for 268 acres and the other for 150 acres for a total of 418 acres. This would seem to reflect the two tracts that were inherited from his mother, although it does not reflect the 1850 purchase of 100 acres on Walker's Creek in a land grant from the state of North Carolina.[47] Additionally, he remarked in the suit that he acquired these two tracts five or six years before (approximately 1850-51). This would also indicate that he was referring to the inherited land, since both Healy and Miles were dead by then, with Miles having died in June 1850. However, his remarks do not seem to reflect the 1851 deed where he relinquished claims to this land. Regardless of how he acquired this land it would become collateral to cover his bond and securities in this case.

As a result of the petition, Judge John M. Dick felt that the

---

#0019645.

[44] Emsley and Susan Lassiter et al to Calier Phillips, Deed Book 29:495. FHLM #0470233.

[45] "The Willie Lassiter Petition," *The Genealogical Journal* by the Randolph County Genealogical Society, V, 1 (Winter 1981):38-42.

[46] It is interesting to note that while the petition indicates that he was in the carriage trade, the 1850 census records "painter" as his occupation.

[47] State of North Carolina to Wiley P. Lassiter, Deed Book 23:172. FHLM #0019638 or #0470231.

court had done a "great injustice" by allowing Bingham to recover the seven judgments. He ordered the judge in the original case to submit written documentation of that case and judgment, and ordered Michael Bingham to appear at the next court term to answer the petition. As a part of that process, Wiley was ordered to enter bonds and securities with the court. To do that he took out two deeds of trust with Robert G. Murdock, one on 268 acres of the land, including land along Hannah's Creek and the Walker's Creek land grant,[48] and another on his personal property, including his house.[49]

Unfortunately Michael Bingham died, and in the Spring 1857 session, the Superior Court required Wiley to withdraw his petition, leaving in place the seven judgments against him.[50] This undoubtedly left him in considerable debt, and probably forced him to forfeit the two deeds of trust with Robert Murdock. Apparently having lost everything, Wiley left the county.

Preserved among the documents in Harold Lassiter's possession was a letter written by Wiley to Colier in 1858. It revealed that Wiley and his family were living in Fayetteville. In the letter he mentioned that Jane was also there, helping out.

North Carolina
Fayetteville
August the 10th 1858

Mr Calier Calier Lassiter

dear Brother I rite a fu lines to you to inform you how times are with us I can inform you that too of my family ar at this time doun sick. Bettey is vary lo can not sit up any nor waulk on stepe intirly

---

[48] Wiley Phillips to Robert Murdock, Deed Book 29:471. FHLM #0470233.

[49] Wiley Lassiter to Robert Murdock, Deed Book 30:326. FHLM #0470234.

[50] Willie Lassiter v. Michael Bingham, Spring Term 1857, Minutes of the Superior Court and Court of Equity. FHLM #0470215.

helpelis. too doctters ar atending to them. Bettey was taken vary sudin afu days a go she is gitting better we think this is vary much aginst me stopes me from wark and putting me in debt for doctters feas. I have a hard time hear sis Jane is hear staing with us which is a grate helpe. I cold git no person to helpe us as she dos for les then five dolars a weak sh stas for 75 cents as son as tha git wel a nuf I want to cary my family out in the cuntry sum fu miles if tha cant be any location found for them in randolph tha all want to go back tar when we leaf town or I should has moved out in the country last winter.

I am a bige to work hear until I git all paid that I owe hear and you ar lik to sufer on the a count. Johnsey Cranford inform me that his propaty was blege to be sold on my a count unles I cold rase sum muney for him by the firs of next month pleas Calier to se Jonsey Cranford or git John may to se him as son as you git this letter and tel him to tri and mak sum a rang ment with his dets to give a littl more time I have to jobs of work to do as son as I can git them don I whal send him sum muney under the presant condision I am in I se that I cant rase aney muney fur him as son as I have intended in my condision tha dont wants advance muney until the wurk is done unles I had sum way to make them secure I am going to let sum of my debts stand hear and pay Johnsey and you the first muney that I rase ex septng that I spend for sum thing to eat pleas to se him run home he thinks I am not triing to do aney thing fur him under the preant surcumstances I am confind at home earning nothing until my famley git better of I must make sum other arrangment from the way I am lifing one of my famley cant do aney thing hear to helpe me I wil rit to you again in a short time.

W. P. Lasseter

Thus even after he moved away, Wiley apparently needed ever increasing amounts of money for debts and for doctors' bills, due to poor health (some of which was discussed in the above letter). I was told that in an effort to help him, Colier mortgaged portions of his property and took jobs as a laborer.[51]

The children of Wiley and Elizabeth were not named in the 1893 Superior Court decree that divided the Colier Lassiter Tract as the Estate of Miles Lassiter. There might be two possible reasons for this: 1) the 1851 deed, wherein he sold his rights to the land, and 2) none of these family members had ever lived on the land as tenants in common as the other heirs had done.

11. Elizabeth Ridge was born in 1830 in Randolph County, NC.[52] She reappeared in the Randolph County records in 1870,[53] living in the White House section of Asheboro Township. Included in Elizabeth's household were her daughter Julia A., and sons, Addison B. and Thomas Emery. She died after 1870 in Randolph County, NC.[54]

The absence of a marriage record for Wiley and Elizabeth does not, by itself, have significance. While many marriage records of that period for Randolph County have survived, some have been lost. Wiley and Elizabeth's could be one of those that was lost. However, there is another possibility. Family tradition says that Elizabeth was from a prominent White family. (There was a prominent White Ridge family living in Randolph County). Such a marriage was not permissible. Thus, the mar-

---

[51] Testimony of Kate Lassiter Jones, granddaughter of Colier Lassiter to the author, September 1982.

[52] 1850 US Census, Free Schedule, Randolph County, North Carolina (NAM432-641), 136, Willie Lassiter head.

[53] 1870 US Census, population schedule, Randolph County, North Carolina, Elizabeth Lassiter, Asheboro Township, White House Section, pp. 20-21. NAM #593-1156.

[54] 1870 US Census. Randolph County, North Carolina, population schedule, (NAM #M593-1156), Asheboro Township, 20-21. Last found in 1870 census.

riage may have been common-law and never have been registered at the county courthouse.

Elizabeth was gone again from the records in 1880. Her name never reappeared in Randolph County. She may have died sometime before 1880.

12. Nancy Lassiter, born February 1823 in New Hope, Randolph, NC,[55] and died about 1890 in New Hope, Randolph, NC.[56] She married Calvin Dunson (person 13) about 1851 in Asheboro, Randolph, NC.[57]

Nancy's name first appeared in the census records in 1850, in her father's household. In the 1860 census she was with her husband Calvin Dunson and their children. They did not seem to be living in the same area of the county as the family of her brother Colier, but they were not very far away.[58] In 1870, Nancy, Calvin and family, were enumerated next to Colier and family, indicating that they had moved back to the home area around Lassiter's Mill, probably back to the family farm.[59] In 1880, Nancy was a widow and head of household which now included a grandchild, Willie Dunson.[60] She was not found in the 1900 census.

The lack of a marriage record for Nancy and Calvin Dunson makes it difficult to determine the exact date of their marriage, but a number of factors can be used to determine a time period.

---

[55] Handwritten birth record in possession of Harold Lassiter, See also 1850 US Census, Free Schedules, Randolph County, North Carolina, p. 136, (NAM #432-641), Miles Lassiter, head of household.

[56] Anderson Smitherman, et al v. Solomon Kearns, et UX, Final Decree, Superior Court Orders and Decrees,, 2:308-309, FHLM #0475265., Also recorded in Randolph County Deed Book 248:156. FHLM #0470851.

[57] 1860 US Census, free schedule, Randolph County, North Carolina (NAM #M653-910), p.148., Calvin Dunson, head of household. There is no county marriage record for this couple.

[58] 1860 US Census, free schedule, Randolph County, North Carolina, Calvin Dunson, p. 148. NAM #M653-910.

[59] 1870 US Census, population schedule, Randolph County, North Carolina, Calvin Dunson, New Hope Township, p. 10. NAM #M593-1156.

[60] 1880 US Census, population schedule, Randolph County, North Carolina, Nancy Dunson, New Hope Township, p. 1. NAM #T9-978.

These include the 1860 census which lists children: Emsley age 19 (probably not a son, but a younger brother); Ellen, age 9 (her death certificate says she may have been born as late as 1854); Sarah, age 3; and J. Richard, age 1; and the Court of Common Pleas and Quarter Sessions records a case involving Nancy Dunson against a John Hinshaw in 1858.[61] Details were not included. This is the earliest specific reference to her as Nancy Dunson. In the deed of 1851, recorded in 1855, and in the probate record in Will Book 10, which can be assumed to have been recorded in 1854/1855 she is referred to as Nancy Phillips or Lassiter. However, given the haphazard manner in which this probate appears to have been recorded—without letters of administration, without the proper date for the death or the date of probate, without reference in the court minutes—it was likely that the probate was intended to reflect Nancy as an 1851 heir. It is not surprising, therefore, that her marital status went unnoticed. In the same manner, although the deed was not recorded until 1855, it was nonetheless an 1851 document. Thus, it can be concluded that she probably married between 1852 and 1854.

She met J.G. Hoagin (person 14) around 1859 in Randolph County, North Carolina.[62]

13. Calvin Dunson, born about 1820 in Raleigh, Wake, NC,[63] and died about 1879 in New Hope, Randolph, NC.[64]

Calvin Dunson was not originally from Randolph County, but Wake County, North Carolina. Dunson's had lived in the Wake County, North Carolina area since at least the Revolutionary period. A search of the records there revealed that:

---

[61] Nancy Dunson v. John Hinshaw, 2 November 1858, Minutes of the Court of Common Pleas and Quarter Sessions, FHLM #0470212 or #0019653.

[62] Minutes of the Court of Common Pleas and Quarter Sessions, Nancy Dunson v. J. G. Hoagin, February 1859. FHLM #047212 or #0019653.

[63] 1860 US Census, free schedule, Randolph County, North Carolina (NAM #M653-910), p. 148, Calvin Dunson, head of household.

[64] 1880 US Census, population schedule, Randolph County, North Carolina, New Hope Township (NAM#T9-978), p. 1, Nancy Dunson, head of household.

- In 1834, there was a marriage record for Calvin Dunson and Edy Morgan; [65]

- In 1840, the census showed Calvin as head of household;[66] and

- In 1850 neither Calvin's name nor Edy's was listed on the census for Wake County.

Calvin's name appeared in the 1850 census for Randolph County without Edy's name, and it is assumed that she was dead. He was enumerated in the household of Thomas Dunstin, probably a brother.[67]

Little else is known about Calvin except that he was a blacksmith, that he was listed on the voting list for the delegates to the Constitutional Congress for North Carolina after the close of the Civil War,[68] and that he was reportedly a Native American, probably Saponi, from southeastern Virginia/eastern North Carolina. He apparently died a little before 1880, according to the 1892 estate record created from the land dispute between his daughters. According to it, he had died "about 10 years ago," although he did not appear in the 1880 census and Nancy was listed as a widow.[69]

Nancy is thought to have died approximately 1890/1891. At that time, her daughter Ellen purchased all rights to the Lassiter Tract belonging to her (Ellen's) brother, Harris Dunson and his

---

[65] Calvin Dunson and Edy Morgan, Wake County Marriage Bonds. FHLM #296867.

[66] 1840 US Census, Wake County, North Carolina, Calvin Dunson, p. 136. NAM #M704-374.

[67] 1850 US Census, free schedule, Randolph County, North Carolina Thomas Dunstin, Northern Township p. 175, dwelling and family 179. NAM #432-641 or FHLM #444654, item 2.

[68] Delegates to the Consitutional Convention, 1867, Records of the Bureau of Refugees, Freedmen, and Abandoned Lands, North Carolina, NAM #M843, roll 32:107.

[69] Carol Vidales, "Randolph County Estates: Dunbar-Duty." *Randolph County Genealogical Journal*, xxxv(2):45. Entry: William Dunston – 1892.

wife Phoebe (Farmer).[70] By 1892, Nancy's daughters, Ellen and Adelaide, were involved in disputes over the property,[71] and in 1893 the Superior Court decree was issued. No other direct evidence of her date of death has been discovered to date. Nancy is buried in the Old City Cemetery, in Asheboro, where her name is included on a plaque which reads "Swing Low, Sweet Chariot."[72]

14. J.G. Hoagin. No information known.

15. Jane Lassiter was born 07 January 1825 in New Hope, Randolph, NC;[73] died after 1893 in New Hope, Randolph, NC.[74] A spouse has not been identified. She died 1893/1900, based on the fact that she was named in the 1893 division of the land, but not found in the 1900 Randolph County census, although she could have been living somewhere else. A letter from brother Wiley (person 10) to Colier (person 6) in 1858 indicated that she was with his family in Fayetteville, helping to care for his family who were sick at the time. She was subsequently identified in Rowan County, North Carolina, living as a domestic servant.

---

[70] J. H. and Phoebe A. Dunson to Ellen Smitherman, Deed Book 144:216. FHLM #0470278.

[71] Carol Vidales, "Randolph County Estates: Dunbar-Duty." *Randolph County Genealogical Journal*, xxxv(2):45. Entry: William Dunston – 1892.

[72] Randolph County Cemetery Records, Volume II, Central Section, (Asheboro, NC: Randolph County Genealogical Society) 1997, 26, East Section; Row 14 (2), [large granite marker] "Sacred to the memory of our Faithful Colored Friends...Nancy Dunson."

[73] 1850 US Census, Free Schedule, Randolph County, North Carolina (NAM432-641), 136, Miles Lassiter, head.

[74] Randolph County, North Carolina Superior Court Orders and Decrees (FHLM #0475265), 2:308-309, Jane is listed to receive a share of the land. No record of her has been found after this date.

The Second Generation

Child of Emsley Lassiter and Elizabeth Winburn

- Annie Lassiter (person 16)

16. Annie Lassiter, born 1867 in Ripley, Rush, Indiana;[75] died Aft. 1880.

Child of Colier Lassiter and Laura Ann Williams

- Boy Williams (person 17)

17. Boy Williams,[76] born November 1850 in Randolph County, NC.

Children of Colier Lassiter and Katherine Polk

- Bethana Martitia Lassiter (person 18)
- Spinks Lassiter (person 19)
- Amos Barzilla Lassiter (person 20)
- Rhodemia Charity Lassiter (person 21)
- Ulysses Winston Lassiter (person 22)

18. Bethana Martitia Lassiter, born February 1856 in Lassiter Mill, New Hope, Randolph, NC; died 11 July 1917 in Cedar Grove, Randolph, NC. She married Postell Henley 20

---

[75] 1880 US Census, population schedule, Rush County, Indiana, Ripley, (NAM#T9-0308), p. 62A, Emsley Lassiter, head.

[76] Calyer Phillips Bastardy Bond, Minutes of the Court of Common Pleas and Quarter Sessions, Randolph County, North Carolina, May Term 1851, FHLM #0019652 or #0470212. Bastardy Bonds, 1850-1859, *The Genealogical Journal* by the Randolph County Genealogical Society, Volume XVIII:2, p. 16, North Carolina State Archives call number, C.R. 081.102.5. "Mother Lorey Ann Williams."

Some Descendants of Miles Lassiter   121

Figure 11.3: Kate Lassiter Jones, Aveus Lassiter Edmundson, Leonard Lassiter, Vella Lassiter and Ruth Lassiter Laughlin. Descendants of Colier Lassiter, 1982.

March 1879 in Asheboro, Randolph, NC.[77] They had one child, George Henley.[78]

19. Spinks Lassiter, born 1858 in Lassiter Mill, New Hope, Randolph, NC;[79] died before 1870 in Lassiter Mill, New Hope, Randolph, NC.[80]

20. Amos Barzilla Lassiter, born 04 December 1861 in Lassiter Mill, New Hope, Randolph, NC; died 16 December 1930 in Lassiter Mill, New Hope, Randolph, NC. He married Harriett Phillips 11 May 1882 in Asheboro, Randolph, NC.[81]

---

[77] Randolph County, North Carolina Marriage Registers., 4:69.

[78] 1900 US Census, Randolph County, North Carolina (NAM #T623-1212), S.D. 7, E.D. 90, Sheet 1. Postell Henley, head.

[79] 1860 US Census, free schedule, Randolph County, North Carolina (NAM #M653-910), 148, Colier Lassiter, head.

[80] 1870 US Census. Randolph County, North Carolina, population schedule, (NAM #M593-1156), 24, Colier Lassiter, head. Spinks' name was not found in 1870.

[81] Randolph County, North Carolina Marriage Registers., 4:105 Zill Las-

Figure 11.4: Alice Lassiter Speed and Margaret L. Williams

She was born 01 February 1862 in Randolph County and died 01 March 1942 in Lassiter Mill, New Hope, Randolph, NC. Their children were Blanche, Elizabeth, Harris, Spinks, Alice, and Laura Edna.

21. Rhodemia Charity Lassiter, born 1866 in Lassiter Mill, New Hope, Randolph, NC; died in New York, NY. She married Alexander Adderton 20 September 1883 in Asheboro, Randolph, NC.[82] They divorced and he died 01 June 1917 in Asheboro, Randolph, NC. [83]Their children were Bertha, Mae, Collier, Earl, Lucy, and Donald.[84]

22. Ulysses Winston Lassiter, born 30 December 1869 in Lassiter Mill, New Hope, Randolph, NC; died 26 November 1937 in Lassiter Mill, New Hope, Randolph, NC.[85] He mar-

---

siter and Harriett Phillips.

[82] Randolph County, North Carolina Marriage Registers., 4:111. Rhodemia Lassiter and Alex Adderton

[83] Randolph County, North Carolina, Deaths, 4:206. Alex Adderton.

[84] 1930 US Census Manhattan, New York, New York; Roll: 1563; Page: 9B; Enumeration District: 888; Image: 934.0.

[85] Randolph County, North Carolina, Deaths, 24:307. Winston Lassiter.

Some Descendants of Miles Lassiter

Figure 11.5: Ulysses Winston Lassiter

ried Ora Kearns on 08 September 1892, in Asheboro, Randolph, NC.[86] She was born 29 April 1874 in New Hope, Randolph, NC and died 12 September 1951 in Lassiter Mill, New Hope, Randolph, NC.[87] Their children were Mabel, Novella Anna, William Josiah, Charles Colon, George Ulysses, Lovell, Katherine Martitia Lilly Bernice, Clark Henry, Wade Josiah, Aveus, Leonard, and Harold.[88]

Children of Wiley Lassiter and Elizabeth Ridge

- Abigail Lassiter (person 23)

- Nancy Jane Lassiter (person 24)

- Julian Ann Lassiter (person 25)

---

[86] Randolph County, North Carolina Marriage Registers., 5:79. Winston Lassiter and Ora Kearns

[87] Randolph County, North Carolina, Deaths, 38:207. Ora Lasiter.

[88] 1930 US Census, Randolph County, North Carolina, NARA #T626_1715, Census Place: New Hope, Randolph, North Carolina; Roll: 1715; Page: 9B; Winston Lassiter, head. Retrieved from *Ancestry.com*

- Martha Lassiter (person 26)
- John Lassiter (person 27)
- Addison B. Lassiter (person 28)
- Thomas Emery Lassiter (person 29)

23. Abigail Lassiter, born about 1846 in Lassiter's Mill, New Hope, Randolph, NC.[89] When or where she died is currently unknown. Information from Nephard Hines Harris (granddaughter of Abigail's sister Julia, person 25 below) indicates she married and lived in the Friendship area of Guilford County. She reportedly had a son whose name may have been "Harry." Based on this, she may have been the Abigail married to Clarkson Kearns, with sons named Harrison, McKender, Franklin and James.[90]

24. Nancy Jane Lassiter, born in February 1848 in Lassiter's Mill, New Hope, Randolph, NC and died after 1900. Nancy (using her middle name, "Jane") married Thomas Bryant on 1 October 1868.[91] They were listed in New Hope Academy, New Hope Township in the 1870 census.[92] Nancy's sister Julia (person 25) and brother Addison (person 28) were also listed with them in the 1870 census, probably indicating that they were spending considerable time in the Bryant household. Jane's and Thomas' children were George W., William, and John M.[93]

---

[89] 1850 US Census, Free Schedule, Randolph County, North Carolina (NAM432-641), 136, Willie Lassiter, head.

[90] 1870; US Census, Asheboro, Randolph, North Carolina; (NAM #M593-1156), 284A retrieved from *Ancestry.com*, FHL #552655, Clarkson Kearns, head.

[91] Jane Lassiter and Thomas Bryant, Randolph County Marriage Book 3:42. FHLM #0475241.

[92] 1870 US Census, population schedule, Randolph County, North Carolina, Thomas Bryant, New Hope Township, p. 5, dwelling 40, family 42. NAM #M593-1156.

[93] 1880 US Census, Cedar Grove, Randolph, North Carolina; (NAM #M-978; FHL 1254978); 154B, retrieved from *Ancestry.com,* Thomas Bryant,

25. Julia Ann Lassiter, born May 1852 in Lassiter's Mill, New Hope, Randolph, NC; died 31 January 1921 in Cedar Grove, Randolph, NC[94]. She married Henry Sanders on 18 January 1877, Asheboro, Randolph, NC. [95]Their children were Julius, Mary Martha, Thomas Fred, Lula J, Myrtle M.[96]

Figure 11.6: Julia Ann Lassiter Sanders and daughter, Mary Martha Sanders Hines

---

head; and *see also*, 1900 US Census, Cedar Grove, Randolph, North Carolina; (NAM #T623-1212); 4A, Thomas Bryant, head. Retrieved from *Ancestry.com*.

[94] Randolph County Death Records, Book 8:59; *See also*, North Carolina Death Certificate 503, Register 3, retrieved from *Ancestry.com*.

[95] Randolph County Marriage Records, Book 4:45. Julia Lassiter and Henry Sanders.

[96] 1910 US Census, Cedar Grove, Randolph, North Carolina; (NAM #T624-1128, FHL Number: 1375141). Page: 9B, Julia Sanders, head. Retrieved from *Ancestry.com*.

26. Martha Lassiter, born in 1854 in Lassiter Mill, Randolph, NC.[97]

27. John Lassiter, born in 1857 in Lassiter Mill, Randolph, NC.[98]

28. Addison B. Lassiter, born 1862 in NC.[99] He first married Adelaide Freeman, 22 September 1883 in Randolph County.[100] Adelaide may have died. Addison moved to Pennsylvania, where he married Henrietta Butler.[101] He eventually moved to Barnegat, Ocean, New Jersey where he may have died.[102] Their children were: Addison, Alice E., Henrietta, and Aretta.[103]

29. Thomas Emery Lassiter, born about 1865 in NC.[104] It appears he moved to Washington, DC, married a woman named Alice and apparently died there. Tom and Alice married late in life and had no children.[105]

---

[97] 1860 US Census Fayetteville, Cumberland, North Carolina; NARA #M653-894; Page: 248; FHLM #803894. Dwelling 1087, Family 1022, Wiley Lassiter, Head.

[98] Ibid.

[99] 1870 US Census. Randolph County, North Carolina, population schedule, (NAM #M593-1156), 20, Elizabeth Lassiter, head.

[100] Ancestry.com. *North Carolina Marriage Collection, 1741-2004* [database on-line], 2007.

[101] 1910 US Census, Philadelphia Ward 20, Philadelphia, Pennsylvania; (NAM #T624-1394), 9B; FHL Number: 1375407; Retrieved from *Ancestry.com,* Addison Lassater, head.

[102] 1930 US Census, Union, Ocean, New Jersey; (NAM # M-1375), 3B, retrieved from *Ancestry.com,* Addison Lassiter, Roomer; Mary Geders, head.

[103] Ibid. *See also* 1920 US Census: South Brownsville, Fayette, Pennsylvania; (NAM #T625_1570) 7B, retrieved from Ancestry.com, Addison Lasiter, head.

[104] 1870 US Census. Randolph County, North Carolina, population schedule, (NAM #M593-1156), 20, Elizabeth Lassiter, head.

[105] 1930 US Census. Washington, Washington, District of Columbia; Roll: 294; Page: 20A; Enumeration District: 77, retrieved from *Ancestry.com,* Thomas E. and Alice Lassiter, roomers in the home of Roberta Parker.

Figure 11.7: Julia Ann and Thomas E. Lassiter

Child of Nancy Lassiter and J.G. Hoagin

- J. Richard Dunson (person 30)

30. Richard Dunson, born 1859 in New Hope, Randolph, NC;[106] died between 1860 and 1870 in New Hope, Randolph, NC.[107]

Children of Nancy Lassiter and Calvin Dunson

- Ellen Dunson (person 31)
- Sarah Rebecca Dunson (person 32)
- J. Harris Dunson (person 33)
- M. Adelaide Dunson (person 34)

---

[106] 1860 US Census, free schedule, Randolph County, North Carolina, p. 148, Calvin Dunson, head. NAM #M653-910.

[107] 1870 US Census. Randolph County, North Carolina, population schedule, (NAM #M593-1156), p. 10, Calvin Dunson, head. NAM #M593-1156. J. Richard is no longer listed and is never listed again.

- Martha Ann Dunson (person 35)

Figure 11.8: Roxanne Smitherman Waddell Wilburn

31. Ellen Dunson, born 08 August 1852 in New Hope, Randolph, NC; died 12 June 1920 in Asheboro, Randolph, NC. She is buried in the Oddfellows Cemetery in Asheboro. She married first, Anderson Smitherman. They had Mary Louise, Spinks, Roxanne and Amma. They divorced and she married Charles Mayo.

32. Sarah Rebecca Dunson, born 1857 in New Hope, Randolph, NC; died between 1880 and 1892 in New Hope, Randolph, NC. She had one son, William.[108]

33. J. Harris Dunson, born 1860 in New Hope, Randolph,

---

[108] Carol Vidales, (Summer 2011) "Randolph County Estates, Dunbar-Duty," Entry: William Dunston.

Figure 11.9: Oddfellows Cemetery, Asheboro NC, 1982

NC;[109] died after 1920.[110] He married Phoebe Farmer 03 April 1890 in Asheboro, Randolph, NC;[111] born in Farmer, Concord, Randolph, NC; died after 1891.[112] They had no children.

34. M. Adelaide Dunson, born 1861 in New Hope, Randolph, NC; married Solomon Kearns;[113] and died 09 May 1929 in Concord, Randolph, NC.[114] They had Sula, and Mary

---

[109] 1870 US Census. Randolph County, North Carolina, population schedule, (NAM #M593-1156), p. 10, Calvin Dunson, head. NAM #M593-1156.

[110] 1920 US Census, population schedule, Randolph County, North Carolina, [NAM #T625-1318.], p. 136, Solomon J. Kearns, Concord Township, S.D. 7, E.D. 103, [p. 136], Sheet 10B, farm 190, family 195. Not been found after this.

[111] Randolph County, North Carolina Marriage Registers., Book 5:13., Harris Dunson and Phoebe Farmer. FHLM #0475241.

[112] Randolph County, North Carolina, Deeds, Deed Book 144:216, J. H. and Phoebe A. Dunson to Ellen Smitherman, FHLM #0470278.

[113] Randolph County, North Carolina Marriage Registers., Book 5:17. Solomon Kearns and Adelaide Dunson, FHLM #0475241

[114] Randolph County, North Carolina Deaths, Book 16:161.. FHLM #0475244.

Dicy.[115]

35. Martha Ann Dunson, born 1864 in Lassiter's Mill, New Hope, Randolph, NC; died between 1885-1886 in Lassiter Mill, New Hope, Randolph, NC. She was married briefly before her death to Julius Hill. They had one daughter Mamie.[116]

---

[115] 1900 US Census New Hope, Randolph, North Carolina (NAM #T623-1213) 3B, retrieved from *Ancestry.com*. Solomon Kearns, head.

[116] Carol Vidales. (Summer 2011) "Randolph County Estates: Dunbar-Duty," Entry: William Dunston.

Backintyme
30 Medford Drive
Palm Coast FL 32137-2504
860-468-9631

See our complete list of books at:
http://backintyme.com/publishing.php

Order extra copies of this book at:
http://backintyme.com/ad382.php

www.ingramcontent.com/pod-product-compliance
Lightning Source LLC
Chambersburg PA
CBHW032135040426
42449CB00005B/245